# TUTORING
# AS A
# SUCCESSFUL BUSINESS

## AN EXPERT TUTOR
## SHOWS YOU HOW

**Eileen Kaplan Shapiro**

**Tutoring as a Successful Business**
By Eileen Kaplan Shapiro

Copyright © 2001 by Eileen Kaplan Shapiro

Published by:
Nateen Publishing Co.
P.O. Box 1916
Burbank, CA 91505

ISBN: 0-9672361-0-X
Library of Congress Control Number: 00-91230
Printed in the United States of America
10 9 8 7 6 5 4 3 2 1

**Publications** by Eileen Kaplan Shapiro
*WORDS, WORDS, WORDS*
  *810 of the Most Commonly Used Words on the SAT*
For the Chicago Tribune Educational Services Department
  Pamphlets:
    *Studying: Tips to Save You Time*
    *Ideas To Help You Study*
    *The Student Success Book*
Computer Disks for the College Entrance Exams
  Studying for the SAT: English (1983)
  Studying for the SAT: English (1984)
  Studying for the SAT: Math (1984)

**Page design by One-On-One Book Production, West Hills, CA**

## DEDICATION

*This book is dedicated to Suzie, David, Barbara, and Rob, my wonderful children, from whom I learned how special every child is and how important learning is; to my adored grandchildren: Danny, Jon, Joel, Mara and Anna Wilson; Ben, Ariel, Rebecca, Abby, Emily and Sam Shapiro; and Erik Thiede, who have reinforced my beliefs about children; and most importantly, to my husband, Nate, who, after 50 years, continues to be my greatest love.*

## SPECIAL NOTE

*Suzie Wilson, my daughter, confidante, co-author and teacher par excellence, died of breast cancer in April of 1996. Her students, her friends, every teacher, everyone she touched loved and admired her; she was a fierce advocate for better education, working tirelessly to make sure every child had every opportunity to learn and grow. She is sorely missed and without her presence, the world is a lesser place.*

# ACKNOWLEDGMENTS

I owe an enormous "thank you" to a great many people: to Alma V. Jones, the first principal for whom I taught, for telling me I was an extremely good and caring teacher; to all of the devoted teachers who generously gave me insights into their students whom I was tutoring; and *most importantly* to all of the more than 6,000 students I worked with who made my work challenging and exciting and to all of their parents who put their trust in me. I want to thank Gayle Anne Moschenross for her help typing the original copy and to Jim Moschenross who kept my computer alive and working. I wish to thank Hugh Griffin for his invaluable advice; Dave Wollert for his creative help; and Alan Gadney and Carolyn Porter for their expert handling of the production and marketing of this book. And, once again, a big thank you to my staunchest supporter and "always available" editor, my husband Nate.

# ABOUT THE AUTHOR

**Eileen Shapiro**

Eileen Shapiro's successful tutoring career began in 1972 as a sixth-grade teacher in a Glenview, Illinois Public school located near a U.S. Navy airbase. She soon discovered that many of her students had missed important aspects of previous learning because of their constant movement from one airbase to another. Concerned, she began to volunteer tutor them before classes, on their lunch hours and after school.

Later, after leaving her teaching position and looking to continue her educational work, a friend suggested tutoring for profit. The rest is history!

She has researched and tutored many different subjects and grade levels with outstanding success. Her students have ranged from those in Special Ed and Learning Disabilities classes to gifted learners. She has tutored students from pre-school through high school and taught college students and adults. Her first move with a new student is to locate the place where the student stopped understanding the material and then begin the "re-teaching" from that point on.

Eileen has spoken before PTA meetings and to college-bound student groups as well as appearing on TV interviews. Parents, school counselors and students all praise her work.

Mrs. Shapiro has written a number of well-known educational materials. Among them, two study skills booklets for *The Chicago Tribune*, which distributed a half-million copies to Chicago area elementary and high schools. The *Tribune* also asked her to write a major "stay-in-school pamphlet," the *Student Success Book*, for students thinking of dropping out of school.

She has also created computer disks to help students study for the SAT and ACT college entrance exams. These were sold nationwide.

Together with her daughter, the late Susan Shapiro Wilson, Eileen wrote a SAT dictionary, *Words, Words, Words* containing 810 words most commonly used in the SAT. One of her students memorized the entire dictionary and scored 760 out of a possible 800 on his SAT verbal section. The book has been used in Southern California English classes.

For over 28 years Eileen has tutored more than 6,000 students in virtually all subjects including the SAT and ACT exams. Both public and parochial high schools have hired her to teach the SAT to their students. She has also consulted elementary schools in teaching word problems and shortcuts for math studies.

Mrs. Shapiro is married, has four children and 12 grandchildren. She and her husband Nate live in Southern California.

# TABLE OF CONTENTS

## SECTION I

# SECTION II

# SECTION III

# PREFACE

I wanted to make money, and I wanted to stay home because two of my children were still in school. One day I sat down at my desk and made a list of all the things I was good at. To my surprise the list was quite long. It included painting, sewing, baking, writing and teaching. It didn't take me long to realize there was no money in the first three and the fourth might take some time before editors accepted my material.

However, I loved teaching and had given it up to be home with my four children, one of whom was a toddler. But now two of my children were in college, one was in high school, and my youngest, who was seven, was in elementary school. As I looked at the list, I remembered how much I had loved working with the kids who were having trouble with their classwork. I loved watching their faces light up when they finally understood the concepts and could manage the work. I loved watching their self-confidence grow. I almost shouted "Eureka!" when I realized here was something I could do without leaving home or my children. I could make money too.

There are many reasons why a tutoring business can be an ideal home-based business. There are no large capital requirements; you can borrow books from schools or get them in libraries. You can even write your own material and use games you may have around the house. Playing cards are great for learning numbers.

You can choose your own hours. You may want to teach only from after school hours to dinner time or you may prefer after dinner hours. You may want to teach only on Saturdays. Your working hours are up to you.

**YOU DON'T NEED A CERTIFICATE TO TEACH.** If you are great in math and feel you can really impart that knowledge, then you can teach it. If you love science and understand chemistry or physics, then you can tutor students in those subjects. Look at the many volunteers in the schools without degrees who are helping students every day!

You don't need any special furniture to tutor. A kitchen or dining room table works great and sometimes you may even want to sit on a couch when you're reading with a younger child.

Overall, there is very little overhead to start tutoring. All you really need is to care about people and like to teach. And when people hear about how good you are at your work, word of mouth will spread quickly.

When I began tutoring, I never dreamed that within a few years I would be so busy that I would be working Mondays through Thursdays from 3:00 in the afternoon until 10 in the evening and on Fridays until 6:00. And that a few years later I would add Sundays to my workdays when I started classes for the college entrance exams.

There was no one pushing me to work that hard. I just couldn't say no when parents called. My family gave me wonderful support, and I was thriving.

I started tutoring in 1972. Before I actually put an ad in the paper, I talked to many people who told me I was being foolish. They said parents would never pay $10 for 45 minutes once a week; what would they do if their child needed to see me twice a week? And besides it was May and who would bring their children during the summer months? No, tutoring was done from September to June and only then.

I listened to the naysayers and after a few weeks decided to stop listening. I put an ad in the papers and the same night it ran, the phone rang. A mother asked me lots of questions and then decided to bring her daughter to me . . . twice a week!

I had already decided to tutor in our recreation room. We put the television in an unused bedroom, my son entertained his friends in his room or the living room, and we used the recreation room only on the weekends.

That's how I got started and built a successful, money making tutoring business in my home.

This book will tell you how you can build a successful tutoring business in your home too.

# HOW TO USE THIS BOOK

Each chapter has several suggestions, games, and ideas to use when tutoring.

In the chapter on reading, there is a section about young students who are reading but not remembering what they read. I have included a game using different colored items which they see and then try to remember when the objects are hidden. The game gets progressively harder and reinforces the students' retention.

Playing bingo works in both reading and in math. In reading you just insert the words the kids need to learn and also put them on the flashcards; in math, write in the answers to the math problems you have written on cards. The kids know they are playing "learning" games, but they love it.

There are suggestions for teaching SATs and ACTs (the college entrance exams) and even ideas for performing chemistry "labs" in a home.

Some of the stories and work sheets are too long to put within a chapter so are printed in full in the Appendices section of this book.

These ideas have worked successfully; feel free to use them.

# SECTION I

# Tutoring Will Never Be the Same. . . It Will be *More Fun!*

Chapter One

# The Story of Brad

He was peeking out from behind his mother's skirt, a very small boy with big brown eyes hidden behind thick horned rimmed glasses. His dark hair fell below his eyebrows, and when he saw me, he pressed even closer against his mother as if to become one with her.

"This is Brad," his mother said. "He's almost seven, and he's here to learn to read better."

I knelt down to his level and put out my hand. "Hi, Brad, how are you today? You look like you've been playing outside. Would you like something cool to drink?"

He held his mother tighter. A tiny "yes" squeaked out as he looked around my living room. With a firm grip on his mother's hand, he was turning himself in every direction to explore the room. "Is this where I'm going to learn to read?"

"No," I replied. "We're going to work downstairs in my family room. I have lots of books down there and a blackboard and coloring books and all kinds of interesting things. Would you like to go down and see the room? You can bring your mother too."

So we all went downstairs. I like to let all my new students, whatever their ages, explore my room. They become familiar with it and learn to be more comfortable when working with me.

Brad walked slowly from one end of the 40-foot room to the other, examining my son's beer can collection with oohs and ahs. He looked at all the books, at the television set, the blackboard, the bar. He sat on every chair, on the couch, peeked into every nook and cranny. He struck pay dirt when he saw the remote control switcher for the TV! "What is that? Can I work it? Please?"

So for a very few minutes we worked the "toy." Brad was fascinated. Especially when he managed to turn the set to Sesame Street, a show he enjoyed.

Finally we went over to the table where I worked. Brad was so tiny he could barely see above the edge, so we found a higher chair for him. He saw a *Dr. Doolittle I Can Read Book* on the desk and shouted, "I have that book! I'll read it to you. I can read it all by myself!" And because he knew the plot, he turned each page and told me the story. It didn't take long to find out that he could hardly read. He knew most of his letters and sounds and a few sight words. And so we started his lessons by reviewing all the letters. Mostly we spent the time getting to know each other better.

When we rejoined his mother, I told her he could use a lot of help. When his mother had called me originally, she reported that Brad was in a learning disabilities class, and his regular teacher was thinking of retaining him in the first grade in the fall. He was not only small, but he had a late birthday, making him one of the youngest children in the class.

I asked his mother for time. I told her I didn't believe in keeping children back at such a young age. They all learn at different rates, maybe just reading first and later math, or vice versa, though some can learn both at the same time.

I also explained that as failing or getting low grades becomes a thing of the past, students see that they can do what they always thought was impossible. And their self-confidence begins to grow. "Look at me," they'll beam. "I can do anything!"

And as a result, that self-confidence spills over into all their relationships. Many parents, I said, had told me they couldn't get over the change in their children. The youngsters were less frustrated, less argumentative, and generally easier to live with.

# The Story of Brad

And the teachers had told those same parents what remarkable changes they had seen in the children. The students were joining in class discussions and answering questions instead of just sitting in class daydreaming. The students themselves told of making new friends and enjoying social situations. I believed that Brad could achieve what was expected of a second grader by the end of the year, if he just had some extra help.

That evening his mother called. She and her husband had decided to keep Brad in second grade, stay with his learning disabilities teacher, and bring him to work with me.

In the beginning when Brad arrived, it took us ten minutes or so to get started. He had to explore the room, play with the things in it, or tell me everything that was happening in his life at that moment. He talked about his dog or about Star Trek, his favorite TV show. He constantly looked at the beer cans, turning each one as he ran his fingers over the letters as if to let me know how much he would like to have one. And when he finally did sit down, I could hold his attention for only a little while before his mind wandered. It was "pull and tug" in a caring but extremely tiring way.

Sometimes, after he left, I would sit down and wonder why I had chosen teaching as my career. I felt now and then as if I were knocking my head against a brick wall — that time was stacked against me. His regular teacher saw him 30 to 35 hours a week. His learning disabilities teacher saw him every day. How was I supposed to get through to him in just 45 minutes a week?

One day I was sorting out some of my daughter's things and came across two trophies she had received for drama in high school. I put them out on the shelves. Naturally Brad saw them immediately. He knew trophies were awards and he wanted to know whose they were, what they were for, and if he could have one. After listening (patiently!) to my whole explanation, he put them down slowly.

"Someday," he said, "I'd like one. But I don't play ball with the guys yet. They say I'm not good enough. And I can't win any races 'cause I'm too small. And I don't win anything in my class. I wish I could have one."

I swallowed the lump in my throat. Here was this little boy who so wanted to be good enough to be accepted and to be liked. His shoulders drooped just thinking about it. It was then that I decided what I would get him for his birthday: a trophy, duly inscribed. I wanted him to feel special, to feel that he was someone! So when the time came, I ordered a small trophy, inscribed, "TO BRAD — FOR BEING A GREAT STUDENT!" His mother told me later that when he opened the gift, his eyes almost popped out! He was ecstatic!

That fall, Brad began to make progress. I praised him every time he learned a new phonetic sound or recognized a new sight word. Over and over I told him what a terrific student he was! Even when he found it difficult to understand a concept, I encouraged him, saying I could see how hard he was trying.

He gradually learned to concentrate for longer periods of time. And he was beginning to get along better with his classmates and was starting to try new activities during recess.

Fall turned to winter and I began to feel that he should move more quickly. Spring was only four months away, and I had predicted that he would be almost caught up by then. He was reading sentences now, simple ones, but oh, so slowly.

Then one day, he casually opened a book and began to read aloud to me! I nearly fell off my chair! "I learned to read in school today," he said proudly, not remembering all the extra time we had been putting in.

I called his teacher. She was happy with the progress he was making. Now if only he could do his math.

# The Story of Brad

So we started working in that area. We didn't stop studying reading comprehension, but we made math our major focus in every session. Brad was having all kinds of trouble regrouping. If the problem was 24 minus 16, why couldn't he just subtract the 4 from the 6 and then the 1 from the 2? "Don't you always take the smaller number from the larger one?" He'd bite his lip, frown, and his big brown eyes showed his bewilderment.

I tried everything. I drew pictures. I counted out cards and put them in piles; I cut strips of papers. Nothing seemed to penetrate. Still I kept telling Brad how great he was, how well he was learning. "You'll learn this, Brad," I'd say. "I've seen you work and try. One of these days, you'll surprise yourself and start subtracting and then you'll wonder why you ever thought it was so hard. You'll see."

And then one beautiful spring afternoon, Brad raced into my house and blurted out, "I've got a secret! I'll tell you when we get to our table." He could hardly contain himself. "Guess what happened to me today? The guys asked me to be the pitcher on their baseball team!" Brad was stretching tall and pretending to pitch. Then he stood straight up. "And I learned how to subtract, and I got 100 on my paper!"

One look at the broad grin on his face told me all I had to know. Brad had it all together. He was on his way! And I was proud to know that I had helped it happen.

## Chapter Two

# An Overview of Tutoring

"Tutoring? Who ever made any real money tutoring? It's pin money — no more than that!" This is what most people think. But, they're very much mistaken.

You can make very good money tutoring, and you can make that money in your own home. And times are changing. Until recently, many mothers and fathers who are bright, qualified teachers went outside their homes to pursue their careers. They either took their own children to day-care centers or gave them keys to the house, making them the "latch-key" kids who came home to an empty house. Today, many of these parents, mothers and fathers, want to stay home with their children. Just as these parents are deeply committed to their own children's education, so are they still committed to the education of all children. But how can these parent/teachers stay home and still teach? By tutoring. By using their love of teaching to help those students who need special help in school, those who are studying for college entrance exams, and even those who are gifted and very possibly bored in their regular classes.

And what if you are not a certified teacher but are well qualified and love to teach? When I was 15, I taught my younger sister to read when she was five years old. Long before I returned to college for my teacher's degree, I taught my own children to read and add when they were four and five years old. Every time you explain a "how, what, why, where, or when" question, you are teaching. Every time you point out something new, you are teaching. You see, *anyone* can tutor.

# An Overview of Tutoring

There has never been a better time to be a tutor than now. Headlines in newspapers are screaming that there is trouble in the schools! Students are not getting enough of the basics. Or they are falling behind in math and science. Students can't get jobs because they can't write, or if they can write, they can't spell. Geography has become a subject of the past. A recent survey showed that many college students don't know where well-known cities or countries are located. And high school students are finding that it is becoming much harder to get into the colleges they want to go to.

If all this weren't enough, we have a president who says he cares about education. He wants our children to have better educations, to be better prepared for the future.

You may say, "Oh, but that's not the case where I live. We are known to have some of the best schools in the country."

Well, that is what many people are led to believe. But I tutored in Chicago for 20 years in an area where there are many wealthy people, where most of the residents are professionals: doctors, lawyers, accountants, etc. I have tutored the past ten years in the San Fernando Valley in Los Angeles where again many professionals live.

We have highly paid teachers, implying that we have the best, most caring teachers. But is that true? Without a doubt, there are some wonderful teachers, who, day after day, impart knowledge in a meaningful and productive way. They ask probing questions; they stir students' imaginations; they stimulate ideas. They are the excellent teachers.

On the other hand, there are too many apathetic teachers, the ones who arrive at 8:00 and leave promptly at 3:00. "I don't understand why you can't learn this," they'll say. "I explained it once already." Or, "Stay after class and show me what's bothering you." *Stay after class when a student has only three minutes to get to his next class which may be half way across the school?* And if the

9

student does have those few minutes free, will that be enough time? What happened to the teachers who say, "Ask questions in class and keep asking until you understand"?

And do you have any idea how many teachers are saying, "Enough questions. This is how it's done, so do it this way." No explanations, no reviewing. And when almost an entire class fails a test, the teachers say, "This is terrible, and as your teacher, I'm embarrassed!" Embarrassed? They should be *ashamed.* If that many kids are failing, the teachers are obviously doing something wrong! Either they are giving impossible tests or they are teaching their subjects in a way that makes the material almost impossible to understand. Perhaps you are thinking, "I've heard all of this. But how can I believe that what you are saying goes on in our schools is really so?"

Well, you only need to spend one week with me, sitting next to the students I tutor and listening to them. Their experiences and comments will prove what I am saying is true, and that there is a crying need for good tutors.

☆  ☆  ☆

Mrs. Pappas called me the morning after a parent-teacher conference. She sounded very upset. "My daughter Wendy is in the 7th grade," she said, "and last night, her math teacher told me that Wendy is falling far behind the class. My daughter is already in the lowest math group, but what confuses me is that last summer, before she entered junior high school, we sent her to summer school so that she'd be well prepared when school began. She had the very same teacher then as she has now and all summer that same teacher gave Wendy A's and B's. She even said Wendy was a very good math student. How could things change so much in just a few months?" Mrs. Pappas asked if I could see Wendy, talk to her, look at her old math papers and then figure out what was happening.

We made an appointment, and I met with her daughter. Wendy was a tall attractive girl and smiled as she walked in. We sat down, and after asking several questions, I discovered that Wendy's teacher reviewed any new work very quickly and then could not tolerate too many questions after her explanations. I also found out that this teacher began every class period with a short timed test: 10 problems made up of addition, subtraction, long division, and multiplication. Because Wendy wanted to finish every test on time, she made careless mistakes.

I looked at her *regular* test papers. Wendy made some careless mistakes, but she also made errors because she didn't understand the work; she had a very hard time with long division. Her teacher made large red marks over the wrong answers, wrote in the correct answers, but offered no explanations about where the errors were made. Here, it appeared, was a teacher who was losing a potentially good math student because of her own apathy.

It took a few weeks of working together, but soon Wendy was back on track. A few months later, her mother called to say Wendy had been moved into the next higher math group and was doing well.

☆ ☆ ☆

Nan was in the 8th grade in a pre-algebra class. I had helped her brother prepare for the college entrance exams, so I recognized her mother's voice when she called. "I'm so angry," Mrs. Nichols began, "that I don't know what to do anymore. Nan's teacher hands out assignments with no explanations other than to read what is in the book, and everyone in the class is failing. When I go to see him, all I hear is that the kids should understand the work — 'After all, it's in the book and we must move on in order to finish the book by the end of the year!'

"Nan's not in the top math group," Mrs. Nichols continued, "but her class is getting the same assignments as the top group. I've decided that when Nan goes to high school next year, she'll have to take algebra over again. Isn't this a waste of a year!"

Nan and I worked every Tuesday and Friday on her homework. One day she said, "Do you know that I'm the only one getting A's and B's? My teacher knows I see you, but he doesn't care. And the other kids say it doesn't matter because they're all going to retake algebra next year anyway."

It's sad. An entire class losing a whole year because a teacher won't take the time to explain slowly and carefully enough so his class can understand and learn the concepts. What a waste!

☆ ☆ ☆

Many years ago, I began tutoring high school juniors for the Scholastic Aptitude Test (SAT) and the American College Test (ACT), the college entrance exams. Invariably the first questions students always ask are, "Why do I have to take either or both of these tests?" and "I have a high GPA score. Isn't that good enough?"

And the answers are always the same. "Having a high GPA is great. Unfortunately, GPA ratings are scored differently in many schools making it hard for colleges to judge the applicants. Some schools give extra points for AP classes. What a top score of 5 is for them is a 4 to other schools.

"Secondly, every student who is planning to go to a four year college takes these tests. The higher your scores are, the more chances there are of getting into the 'good schools,' and the more choices of 'good schools' there are."

Preparing for the tests is extremely helpful. Students learn what the testmakers want them to know, and they become more confident as the test date approaches.

If you put enough effort and caring into tutoring, and if you can find and fill in those spotty areas, many students and parents will talk about their children's successes and give you great references. Others then will hear about you and call and ask for your services. You can become a highly successful tutor who is very well paid!

## Chapter Three

# The "Can't Read" Kids

It's hard to believe, but after all the weeks of planning and advertising, a student who is having trouble with reading is about to arrive and suddenly you feel a little shaky. What if you can't tell what's wrong? How will you know where to begin? Most anyone can open a book, listen to the children, and correct a word when they read it wrong. But what if the difficulties are more complicated than that?

Here are some systems that helped me diagnose the problems of the students who came to me for help. These systems will work for you too.

## Determining a Student's Reading Level in Elementary School

Suppose students with reading problems come to you for help. First, talk with the children about what they like to do, their families and friends, and show them around your office — anything that will help make them more comfortable with you.

Secondly, determine the level at which they read. You can use printed tests, but if children have been tested too many times, they may turn off and not care about the doing the best they can. You need this information, so if it hard to determine, ask the students if their teachers divide the classes into reading groups. If they do, ask how many groups there are, which group they are in, how often they get to read aloud, and if they know the name of the books they are using. Their answers will help you determine how well or poorly they read.

If they cannot answer your questions, you will have to find their reading levels in another way. Have them read from books written at their grade level. Watch for errors, like stumbling over words or reading without comprehension. If this happens, use a book written at a lower level.

As your students talk about reading, watch their faces. If they read poorly, the sad looks on their faces, more than any spoken words, will tell you how bad they feel about their low status in the class.

Very young children, just learning to read, may have fallen behind for various reasons. They may have moved to a new school where the curriculum is more advanced than the previous school; they may have been ill and missed school; they may just be a little slower in learning to read than some of their classmates. Some of these youngsters really believe they're reading when they find a story they know and tell it to you.

Patsy was turning six when she came to me. She had just moved into a new neighborhood and the children going into first grade were already reading simple sentences. Patsy knew only her letters and sounds.

She bounced into my office, looked at all the reading books and found a copy of a Sesame Street book she had at home. "Oh, look, Grover!" she squealed with delight. "I can read that story already. I'll show you!"

She climbed onto the chair and opened the book. "Do you know what, Mrs. Shapiro? This book has a monster in it. Watch. You'll see it at the end of the book!" And she began to tell me the story.

As she turned each page, she told me what was on it. "Guess what is on the next page?" she asked. "Oh, look how scared Grover is getting! Just wait, Mrs. Shapiro, and see what Grover does!" Her voice got more excited as she neared the end. On the last page, she nearly jumped out of her chair! "See, the monster was Grover all the time! Did you enjoy my story? Didn't I tell you I could read it?"

☆  ☆  ☆

Her delivery was perfect. Her comprehension was great. All Patsy needed was to learn to read! And in four months, Patsy was reading at the same level as her classmates.

Patsy wanted to read. Other students will tell you that they're bored and don't like to read. They say, "The teacher never calls on me," or "Our reading group doesn't meet very often." They won't admit that they are having any difficulties, but they usually sound very unsure of themselves. They try to cover it up, though, and will talk to you about anything else to avoid direct discussion about their reading. It is very important to determine their attitude about reading as well as their reading level.

## Testing Literal and Interpretive Comprehension

Where do you start? Have your students read, either silently or orally, a passage which you feel might be at their reading levels. When they are finished, tell them to close the book. Ask questions about the passage, questions that will test literal comprehension, interpretative thinking, and the ability to draw conclusions. Here is an example of a typed paragraph you can use to see what students can do:

> Jane and Jack decided to go skating on a brook. They didn't see the danger sign nearby. As they skated toward the middle of the brook, there was a loud cracking sound. Someone called out in a very loud voice, "Turn around and come back quickly!" When Jack and Jane were safe, they looked at one another and said, "We sure learned a good lesson today!"

Have them read the story. Then ask questions. "Where were Jack and Jane going and what did they plan to do?" and "On what part of the pond did Jane and Jack skate?" These kinds of literal questions test the students' abilities to retain exactly what they have read, the actual words that appear in the story. The answers are spelled out for the readers.

When you test for interpretative thinking or "decoding," you are asking the students to "read between the lines." For example, "Are the children roller-skating or ice-skating? And what time of the year is it?" Your students should know that one cannot roller-skate on a pond. Why not? Because if it is summer, they'll drown, and if it is winter, the roller-skates won't work. The wheels will get rusty or stick to the ice. So, one ice-skates on a pond in the winter.

Here is another question for interpretative thinking: "How should Jack and Jane have known the ice is thin?" Answer: The danger sign would mention that fact. "So why didn't Jack and Jane know the ice was thin?" They didn't see the sign.

Having tested literal and interpretative thinking, the last type of question, the one that tests the ability to draw conclusions, could be, "What lesson did Jack and Jane learn that day?" Answer: They would be more careful in the future, and they would look at every sign to see if there was any danger.

These kinds of questions can be asked whether your students are reading silently or orally. Oral reading may relay other important clues. You will be able to evaluate word-recognition skills, that is, sight reading and phonetic reading. You will be able to hear poor phrasing skills, tension in their voices, and whether they use any expressions when they read. Do they stop at end of the sentence? Or do they, as many poor readers do, stop at the end of every line? Can they differentiate between a statement and a question? For example:

> Mary watched as her mother, who had been acting strangely, put the milk and bread away. Mary thought to herself, "Why didn't mother buy the rest of the food we need? She's looked so tired and upset lately, I wonder if anything is wrong."

If your students read all of this in a monotone, they may not understand that Mary is concerned that something may be wrong. Show students how important words and punctuation are to a story; words like worried, tired, and upset. Punctuation makes it easier to grasp the meaning of the story too.

## Reversing Letters

Listen for any errors your students might make such as reversals: "was" for "saw" or "how" for "who." Young readers quite often make these kind of mistakes, but usually they are cleared up by third grade. If the errors continue during the third grade, you must continually stop the students after such slips, repeat what they just read, and ask them if the sentence makes sense with the word they had used. Most of the time, when your students see their errors and realize that the sentences are not clear, you can help them figure out their mistakes. If possible, have them sound out the word. If they are having difficulty, don't frustrate them. Tell them what the word is.

One way to help them is to ask questions orally to which the answers contain those dreaded words. For example, "Whom did you see at the party?" Their answer will likely begin, "I saw ....."

Then have them write out the questions and the answers that they gave. Do this repeatedly and soon your students will be on the lookout for those confusing words and make the errors much less often, if at all.

## Adding or Omitting Words

Be sure to watch for omissions or additions of words that may or may not change the meaning of the sentence. If these words change the meaning, stop your students and ask them to reread the sentence. Does their word make sense in the sentence? Are they aware of having added or omitted a word? Explain how one word can change the meaning or thought of the sentence. Occasionally the addition or omission of very minor word makes no difference so just ignore that slip.

## Rereading

There are various reasons for rereading, two of which are very common, and you can determine which of them is causing trouble for your students.

Do your students repeat phrases in sentences or paragraphs to be sure of what they have read? These are some possible answers for this problem: a very bad habit or uncertainty.

If it is only a bad habit, it can be overcome by having the students read a passage without repetition. This may take them a few times. Then ask questions about what they have read. They usually discover that they do remember.

If your students are old enough, time their reading with and without rereading and then show them how much time they are losing by indulging in a habit they can't afford to keep. Habits are hard to break, but once broken are usually gone forever.

The second common reason: they reread because they are uncertain of what they have read. Ask them to read the passage a little more quickly, without rereading. Again they may have to try this a few times. Once they do, make sure they understand and remember the material.

Explain to older children that when they reread, it's very easy to lose the thought or flow of the sentence. It also will hinder them from grasping the meaning of the whole paragraph or passage.

## Differences in Interpretation

You must remember that children think differently. Mark had just finished a passage that talked about wagons traveling on dirt roads across the mountain so was given a worksheet. He was to fill in the correct word in a sentence chosen from words printed on the bottom of the page. One of the sentences read, "The road across the mountain was _____ " Among the choices were "rough" and "straight." Mark chose straight. The teacher's book said that the right word was rough. Who was to say that Mark was wrong?

Another example: There was a map of a city on a page. Down the left side of the map was a river, but down the left side of the city itself were stores along the waterfront. A question was asked "What is on the left side of Park City?" And Mark answered, "On the left side of the city are lots of stores." Again, according to the teacher's book, he should have said, "The river." But he saw the map differently...not incorrectly, just differently.

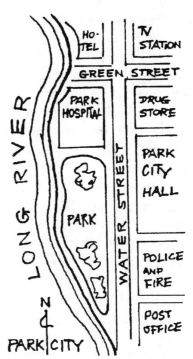

Listen to the answers the students give you. It's surprising, and sometimes very clever, the way their minds work!

**Eileen Shapiro**

# When Unfamiliar Words Puzzle Readers

As your students read to you, check their knowledge of vocabulary words. When books are written, the editors cannot always consider every child's environment.

One of my students, whom I'll call Betsy, has always lived in the suburbs. Naturally, what she knows is what she sees. She knows that her mother does the laundry in her own machines in her own home. She also knows that the cleaning man comes to the house to pick up the cleaning although sometimes her mother takes the cleaning to him by car. The streets are all paved and smooth, and the area she lives in is quiet.

In a story Betsy and I were reading together, a woman had to go to the Laundromat. She needed to wash clothes, but a man who lived in the crowded apartment house was using the machine in the basement laundry room. So she put her clothes in a wagon to take to the Laundromat. Along the way, the wagon tipped over into a very deep rut in the street, and her soiled clothes flew every which way.

A puzzled look came over Betsy's face. When I asked her what was wrong, she answered in a plaintive voice, "I don't know what they're talking about. Where is this lady taking her laundry and why is it in a wagon? And what's a rut anyway? I just don't understand at all!"

Of course, Betsy didn't know. How could she? There was never any need for her to go to a Laundromat. The word wasn't even in her vocabulary. And ruts? How many of those do you see in a nice, residential area? Remember, children in different areas have different vocabularies.

Urban children who live in disadvantaged areas may not understand what a patio or a garbage disposal is. And imagine the confusion on the faces of foreign born children who are learning to read English. They have more than a language barrier. Some may have never seen a television set or a shopping mall. Therefore, make sure you listen to see if your students understand what they are reading. It may seem as though they are having difficulties learning to read, but they may simply be confused because of unfamiliar words.

## Reading Directions

Do your students read directions? You can use workbooks to find out. You may be very surprised at some of the things you'll learn. Some students glance at a page similar to one they've done before and immediately conclude, "I'm supposed to draw a line from the sentence to the correct picture." Because these pages look so much like the ones before, they assume that the directions on the new worksheet must be the same as on the previous pages. So they don't read the directions.

It is also possible that students don't understand the directions. Billy could not read the word "paragraph" so he did the work improperly. "Fill in the missing words" may be misinterpreted. Students may think they can add any word that will complete the sentence, ignoring the selection of words at the bottom of the page.

Students may be very direct and tell you that they don't understand the directions. There are ways to teach a student to read directions. Years ago I found a worksheet that goes something like this:

Answer the following questions as quickly as possible. Read *all* the questions before you begin.

1. Is "mooses" the plural of moose?
2. $9 \times 7 + 2 =$
3. Name the vowels.
4. Which is correct: "she don't" or "she doesn't"?
5. Go to the window and shout out, "Who goes this way?"
6. Divide the word "comfortable" into syllables.
7. Name the nine planets.

8. What is the antonym for apprehend?

9. Write your name in this space _____.

10. How many months have 30 days?

11. Bend over and touch your toes.

12. Spell your name backwards.

13. Do only numbers 2, 3, and 9.

Did you read all the questions before you began, as the instructions said?

There are too many students who gloss over directions and then find they are doing much more work than they have to.

And then there are math pages filled with rows of problems and above the top row on the left side is the simple word, "Add." Further down the page, perhaps above the middle row, is the word, "Subtract." There are no signs of any kind, addition or subtraction, printed with each problem. If students miss that word "subtract," they'll do their work in an indifferent manner and continue adding all the problems on the page. Some are in such a rush that they work hurriedly to finish without seeing the change in direction. And then they wonder why they get such poor marks on their papers! Children catch on pretty quickly when they see how costly it is when they ignore directions.

## Remembering What Is Read

What if your students are reading beautifully and you feel there is no problem — until you ask a question and they give you a blank look?

Dick was in second grade. He was a whiz at math. He could have been in third or fourth grade the way his mathematical mind worked. He read with hardly any mistakes at all, and yet he consistently was in the lowest group. Dick told me that he could hardly ever answer questions about what he had just read. It was my responsibility to discover why that was.

# The "Can't Read" Kids

One day I asked Dick to read aloud one page with six lines of a story. Then I asked him questions about what he had read — the names of the characters, for example. He couldn't remember! Only six lines and he didn't know what was in them! It was no wonder that he could not answer the questions.

To correct this problem, gather together a few things like a small ball, a miniature car, a golf tee, and a crayon. Show them to your students and then ask them to close their eyes while you take away one of them. Your students will have to remember what is missing. Gradually add to the number of items you are using, and then hide one or two more each time.

When students become quite adept at remembering the six or seven different items that are missing, change them. This time, use objects that are alike only in different colors, such as seven crayons or buttons.

Once students remember which of the colored items are missing, place the toys in a certain order. When you feel they have studied them long enough, have the children close their eyes while you mix them up. Tell the children to open their eyes and put the objects back in their original order. First, though, show your students that you have the original order written down. That way they can't argue that their order is the correct original one, not yours.

I did this with Dick. It worked. He began to remember everything that he read. He was excited, his parents were thrilled, and his teacher was pleased.

This kind of retention is important because students have to recall what they read from one page to the next. Eventually they *will* remember the whole story.

## Visual Sequencing

Visual sequencing is the ability to look at pictures out of order and then place them in the correct order. It is also reading several lines of story that are out of order and cutting and pasting them in the correct order.

If you have students who need to work in this area, use comic strips. They're great! Cut the pictures apart and have the students put them into the right order. For example, if you have a picture of a dog jumping on his master as his dish is filled with food, another showing the dog eating, and a third showing a happy dog resting near an empty bowl, cut them apart and have your students put them back into the right order. Add to the number of pictures (up to about six or seven) as your students progress.

Once they have mastered this, find or write a six or seven sentence story. Write each sentence on a separate line, but again out of sequence. Have the kids cut the sentences apart and then paste them in the right order.

## Audio-Visual Problems

Cheryl was a second-grader whose sessions with me had to be kept secret.

"Forget college," her teacher had said to the 7 1/2-year-old. "You'll be lucky if you even make it through high school!"

Imagine hearing those words in second grade. Cheryl's mother didn't believe the teachers. If only she could solve Cheryl's problem, her daughter would do fine. It didn't make sense that Cheryl knew all the rules but couldn't read. She was in a learning disabilities class. So, why wasn't more being done? She liked her LD teacher so there wasn't a personality conflict. Cheryl was a lovable little girl who had no self-confidence at all. There had to be an answer somewhere.

When Cheryl walked in, her head was bent over, and her pretty round face was hidden by long dark hair. She sat down on a chair and waited expectantly. I knelt down so that we were eye-level and introduced myself. She knew why she had come to see me, so I asked her if she would like to read along with me a new book I had just bought. It was a shadow picture book about a little boy who had eaten everything in sight, including bicycles, boots, bird cages, and plates filled with spaghetti, and was so sick that he needed to see a doctor. It was hilarious reading and Cheryl didn't mind that I was watching how she read.

It didn't take long to discover that, in order to read unfamiliar words, she needed to say them as she read them. In other words, she needed to hear and say what she was seeing in print. For example, she would see the word "together." I would break the word into syllables, and then she would point to each syllable, and with my help, say it, hear it and then say the whole word. In addition, I gave Cheryl some sandpaper and colored crayons and asked her to print the words on the sandpaper. This gave her the feel of the letters as she drew them. I also had her work with flour. She etched out the words in this medium. These were ways in which she could feel the words as well as see them and say them. Fingerpainting was fun and useful. We tried to incorporate as many of her senses as possible, feeling, hearing, and seeing. If I could have figured out a way to have her taste or smell the words, I would have done that too.

As we worked together, I discovered that she left out small words and endings when she read. She read "houses" as "house," "walked" as "walk." If a sentence said, "Mary walked down the hill to school," Cheryl would say, "Mary walk down hill school."

We would discuss what happened when she left out words. Did she mean to or from school? Was Mary walking now, before or in the future? Slowly she began to realize just how important those little words were so she read a little more slowly to make sure she read them all.

As Cheryl learned new words, I would show her where rules applied and why. And sometimes she would show me. "It's your turn," she'd say, "to sit on the floor while I write words on the board, okay? Now read them and tell me why they sound like they do." She loved being the teacher.

We made bingo cards with sight words which she learned to recognize. We played our own version of hangman, where I gave her clues to the word she needed. A clue might be "This word has a long 'O' sound and is something you sail in." (boat).

At the end of the year, when I was given permission to call her LD teacher, that teacher said to me, "By the way, do you know what Cheryl's problem is?" It seemed that she had not quite identified it yet!

Cheryl went to day camp most of the summer. She needed a break from school. In fall when she returned, we reviewed what she had learned. Her new third· grade teacher was a gem. She wanted to help Cheryl as did I. Because Cheryl liked her LD teacher so much, it was decided to let her continue going there as long as it was during unscheduled class time.

Cheryl was becoming sure of herself and suddenly I found that this child was terrific in math. She understood concepts quickly, caught on to some faster methods I showed her, and was able to move ahead of many of her classmates. She also moved from the lowest reading group to the one just above that. She did not read smoothly, still leaving off endings and forgetting small words, but she could figure out many new words by herself.

One day, during this third grade year, Cheryl asked if I thought it was possible for her to go to college. "Sure, why not?" I answered. "Anything you want to do, you can do. If that's what you want, you'll do it." She then asked if she would have to go to a special school to be a teacher because she wanted to work for me. Don't think I wasn't flattered! I told her that I'd always have a place for her if she did decide to become a tutor, and I meant it. I also told her that someday she might decide she'd rather do something else. She had trouble understanding that.

Cheryl was becoming more social and playing with more children and she was enjoying school. She continued to see me through the next few years. We only met once a week, but it buoyed her confidence to hear repeatedly how great she was doing. And she was really doing *great*. She only needed a little help. Then one day she entered junior high school, and she was scared. How would she do? When the first report cards came out, Cheryl had average to above average grades. She was meeting many new friends, going to parties, and having a fine time.

One day, she stopped working and was very still. Then she said quietly, "Mrs. Shapiro, when I go to college, I may not be a teacher after all. There are so many other choices I can make." And then she laughed cheerfully. "I guess I am as good as you say I am!"

It has been many years since I worked with Cheryl and when I last spoke with her mother, she told me that Cheryl was in college, working towards her teacher's degree!

## Auditory Sequencing

Auditory sequencing refers to reading a story aloud to the children and then leaving out the ending. Have they followed along so that they can figure out what has happened?

To tutor students who need help in this area, you can tell a story similar to this:

A little girl had seen a sweet potato vine and wanted to grow one herself. So she cut a sweet potato in half crosswise and stuck several toothpicks into one of the cut sides. She then placed the cut side into a glass of water so that the bottom side was continually wet. Every day she watched to see if the vine was growing. Every day she checked to make sure the water was still covering the bottom of the potato. But nothing happened. Every day she made sure the glass was

in the sunlight. She checked that plant every day.
And then one day, she became very excited!

Ask your students if they can tell you what was so exciting. Students really have to listen so that they can come to the correct conclusions.

When you have determined your students' reading levels, choose different reading books from the ones they are using in their classrooms. Why? Because if they read to you from the same book that is in class, they'll become very bored in school. Why read the same story twice? It is much better to use another text written at the same level. That is why it is so important to have many books and materials to choose from.

## Reading Placement Tests

If, after reading this chapter, you still have trouble placing your students at the right level, there are several publishers who sell reading placement tests. You can ask your students' teachers if they can help you locate them, or you can write to textbook publishers and ask them to send you their catalogs that include test books.

## Tutoring Junior and High School Students

I have concentrated mainly on elementary school readers. But there are junior high and high school students who also have trouble reading. Much of the time their difficulties lie with comprehension and vocabulary. What is the author trying to say? Is there a message in the story? And why are some stories so hard to read?

Ask these older kids how they feel about reading, and too many of them will say, "I hate it!" Ask them why and you'll hear, "It's boring" or "The stories are too long" or "I don't care about this stuff so why do I have to read it?"

You can help these kids to read by giving them articles or short stories that interest them, ones about sports, movies, cars, rock stars — anything that will hold their attention. Then discuss what they have read. If possible, add any information that is not in the articles or stories. The students usually love to talk about things they are interested in.

After a time, give them a short book to read, remembering to discuss it first. Arouse their curiosity; make them wonder how things will work out.

Joanne, one of my high school students, had to read *Silas Marner,* and she dreaded it. She had started to read the book but felt the first few chapters were very dry. When she came for her lesson, I gave her hints of what was to come: Silas Marner finds a beautiful child seemingly without a home and decides to raise her; he has gold pieces which he hides; and then in a mysterious and awful way loses them.

Joanne became intrigued. The book played like a soap opera. She decided to start reading the book again and discover what happened to Silas Marner, to his money, and most importantly, to the golden haired child he had raised. And Joanne wanted to know if Marner ever found out who she really was.

The further Joanne got into the book, the more curious she became. After she had read through half of the book, she began to carry it everywhere she went. And when she had finished the book, she told me that she had really enjoyed reading it.

You'll find that although some students won't always have the same reactions as Joanne, many will.

## Vocabulary

Vocabulary is very important, and most students have poor ones. Make that an essential part of your tutoring. One of the best ways to start is to teach prefixes, suffixes and most importantly, root words, a few at a time.

For example: *ami* means friendly; *bel* means angry or warlike. Write sentences using these words, but leave blanks where the words should go. Remember to give choices:

The convict appeared before the judge with a defiant and_____ scowl on his face.

**A.** crafty  **B.** felicitous  **C.** belligerent  **D.** sheepish
**E.** poignant.

If they have studied the roots, they know that C is the correct answer. Remember, too, to tell your students that the word "and" connects two words that are alike in meaning.

Teach your students to look for words that change ideas—words similar to "but, although, however, in fact." What follows is simplistic but gives you the idea. "We all believe that slavery was the only cause of the Civil War. In fact, the South was importing from England the same kinds of equipment that were manufactured in the Northern section of the union. The Northern states were angry. They felt that the Southern states were betraying them."

Explain to your students why they should look for cause and effect in the stories, and to determine what the turning point, the climax, is. Rebuild the excitement your students felt when they were youngsters just learning to read.

There are some excellent books written for junior high and high school students who cannot read at grade level. Again there are several ways to find the right books: ask teachers, look in catalogs, or go to the library. Used book stores often have a few texts that you might be able to use. The stories are shorter and written so that they are easily understood. Publishers print reading books together with workbooks that contain material expressly written for reluctant readers and/or the slower students. These books contain stories that appeal to them. The accompanying workbooks always contain questions on comprehension, spelling, vocabulary, and sometimes grammar. The workbooks occasionally ask students to write out their answers in paragraph form, thereby giving them experience in thinking through the answers before committing them to paper.

## Conclusions

Students, older or younger, who need tutoring usually have the same kinds of difficulties. You can apply all these systems to any of your students. It's easy to implement these ideas, and when you realize your success rate, you'll become even more confident and self-assured.

## Chapter Four

# Tutoring Math

K urt walked slowly into my office. His face drooped, his shoulders sagged, and all in all, he looked like a 14-year-old already beaten by life. He was a thin, dark-haired boy who looked like all it would take to knock him over was the weight of his seventh grade math book.

"It's math," he muttered. "I don't get it. When the teacher starts explaining, I'm O.K. Then, after a few minutes, I'm lost." He sat down, shuffled his feet, and continued muttering. "Big deal, so who needs math anyway?"

"We all do, Kurt, in lots of ways...when we shop, go to the movies, or go out for burgers. May I ask you why having trouble in math is giving you so much grief?"

"It's my folks. They get angry with me and don't understand that I am trying. And my teacher gets mad when I ask so many questions. I must be stupid!"

I looked closely at Kurt's eyes. He was really upset. "Well, I said, "let's see where the problem really is. What are you doing in class right now?"

It turned out that Kurt's class was studying fractions. It was a lower level class, but math was another language to him. He could read any fraction, but the numbers meant nothing. And finding common denominators? Why, that was *really* foreign!

## Starting with the Basics

Students who, like Kurt, are having trouble in math actually began having difficulties long ago. They did not

# Tutoring Math

learn the basic principles in math well enough to build new concepts. No one probably noticed the problems when the children were younger and as the years went by, math became harder and harder. Unfortunately many tutors only work with their students on homework or review only the subject the students are studying. *To be a good tutor is to find where the difficulties first began and then to teach from that point.*

So where to begin with Kurt? I told him I would like to give him a few problems in simple addition, subtraction, multiplication, and division. Starting with the basics would show where Kurt had begun having difficulty. Kurt was very cooperative. (Any students who really want to learn usually will help in any way they can to overcome their problems.) Kurt could add and subtract with ease. But multiply 6 times 8 or 7 times 4? He was lost! Given enough time, he could *add* six 8's. If he couldn't multiply, could he divide? No.

His class was working with fractions. To get some idea of how much he did know, Kurt did some problems with fractions. He knew that 1/2 and 1/4 were less than one, but how much less? Which fraction was larger? And, if he added 1/2 to 1/4, why did he have to change the denominators to be the same? And what were common denominators anyway?

"Okay, Kurt, we're going to backtrack a little. I'll help you with your day-to-day homework, but you need to do a lot of work on multiplication. Somewhere in elementary school, the teachers must not have realized that you were having so much trouble. Otherwise, why would they have just let you go ahead in math? So let's go back and learn the basic skills. Is that okay? It'll take time, but it will be an enormous help to you."

He agreed, but with reservations. It turned out that he had seen many tutors, but they had only helped with the daily homework. Not one of them had tried to discover *why* he had so much difficulty with math.

So that is the road Kurt and I took together. He hadn't learned that multiplication is a shorthand method of addition. He had never learned the multiplication tables "by heart" so that was the first skill he had to acquire. When I told him that learning the tables would help him in division, fractions, and decimals, he realized how important memorizing them were. We worked with concrete items so that he could actually visualize that "three times four" meant three groups of four items, and how many items were there altogether. We drew pictures of three boxes, each containing four candles. We used poker chips, paper clips, pennies, whatever we could find.

Then we worked on another concept: three numbers always go together when multiplying. If 3 times 4 equals 12, then 4 times 3 is 12. No other number multiplied by 3 or 4 could give him 12. And so it was with any three numbers.

After Kurt learned to multiply single digits together, he worked on problems multiplying a number with several digits in it by a single digit. Kurt first learned what positions numbers stood for: 362 means 3 hundreds, 6 tens, and 2 ones. Then in the beginning he learned to multiply like this:

$$
\begin{array}{ll}
\textbf{362 means} & 8 \times 2 = \phantom{00}16 \\
\underline{\textbf{x 8}} & \phantom{0}+ 8 \times 60 = \phantom{0}480 \\
& + 8 \times 300 = \underline{2400} \\
& \phantom{+ 8 \times 300 = }2896
\end{array}
$$

Kurt practiced problems like this several times. When he could do it well, he learned to multiply by regrouping:

$$
\begin{array}{ccc}
362 & 469 & 745 \\
\underline{\text{X8}} & \underline{\text{x7}} & \underline{\text{x9}} \\
2896 & 3283 & 6705
\end{array}
$$

The next step was to do problems like 362 x 93, learning that the 9 was in the 10's place so he had to use a zero as a place holder.

```
    362
  x 93
  1086
32580 (place holder)
```

The final step was multiplying numbers with zeroes in them: 309 x 43 and 639 x 302.

Every math book I have seen says to check answers by reversing the two numbers and multiplying again:

```
   309      then check      43
  x 43                   x 309
   927                     387
 12360                     000
 13287                   12900
                         13287
```

Kurt hated that. When I told him there was an easy and fast way to check his answers, he was delighted. "It takes a little while to understand this," I told him, "but when you catch on, you'll love it."

Multiplication can be checked by casting out 9s:

```
    724
    X57
 41,268
```

**Step 1:**
724 Add 7 + 2 + 4 = 13; subtract multiples of 9: 13 - (1x9) = 4

**Step 2:**
x 57    Add 5 + 7 = 12; subtract all 9s: 12 - (1x9) = 3.

**Step 3:**
Now multiply 3 x 4 = 12; subtract all 9s: 12 - (1x9) = 3

**Step 4:**
41,268 Add 4 + 1 + 2 + 6 + 8 = 21; subtract all 9s: 21 - 18 (2x9) = 3

The answer to Step 3 must equal the "answer" in Step 4. If it does, the problem was done correctly.

**Again** (simplified):

```
    306      3 + 0 + 6 = 9; 9 - (1x9) = 0
  x 238      2 + 3 + 8 = 13; 13 - (1x9) = 4
             0 x 4 = 0
  72,828     7 + 2 + 8 + 2 + 8 = 27; 27 - (3x9) = 0
             0 = 0
```

Kurt understood the procedure in a short while and was excited. He could do something no one else in his class could do.

## Division

Long division was the next problem Kurt had to face. Dividing by two numbers seemed formidable. After his teacher had done several problems with her students, she wrote one on the board for them to do alone.

Kurt was still confused when he came for his next session. I knew he could do short division.

"Well, long division is done the same way as short division except the numbers are larger. You remember:

```
        43
    4)172
       16
       12
       12
```

"With long division you estimate numbers. Try this one: 28)7617. 28 becomes 30, and the first two numbers in the dividend, 76, become 80. 80 divided by 30 is 2. Now use that 2 with the original numbers. 2 x 28 = 56 which you subtract from 76. 76 minus 56 is 20. Continue these steps, remembering to bring down the 1 because 20 cannot be divided by 28."

So Kurt continued, but then with a quizzical look on his face, he said, "I'm stuck. When I estimated 30)200, my answer was 6, but 6 x 28 is 168 and when I subtracted, I got 33 which is too large."

He thought for a minute, and it came to him. "I have to use a larger number. He found that 7 x 28 was 196 and subtracting 196 from 201 left 5. He finished the problem, and it was correct.

```
       271
   28|7616
      56
      201
      196
       56
       56
       00
```

Kurt practiced and practiced and them grinned. "Whew, I'm sure glad I can do long division. It's not too bad after all."

I didn't want to discourage him. "You *are* doing great. However, we haven't worked with zeros yet, and they can sometimes be tricky. Try this: 16|3264."

He did and multiplied 2 x 16 = 32. He subtracted 32 from the 32 in dividend, and he knew he had to bring down the 6. "That's too small. I'll have to bring down the 4." 64 divided by 16 was 4. So he put the 4 in the answer and was proud of himself.

```
       24
   16|3264
      32
      064
      64
       0
```

"Kurt, look at your answer again. There is an important rule you must learn. Once you write the first number in your answer, every number in the dividend must have a number above it. There's no number above the 4. When you brought down the 6, was it divisible by 16? No, So you have to put a zero above it before you bring down the 4."

He studied the work again and saw what he had to do. His answer then was 204.

He practiced several more problems like these and then we added ones that had remainders. Soon Kurt had mastered all the types of long division problems. Then he said, "They're so *easy!*" And we both laughed.

Division, too, can be checked by casting out 9s.

$$\frac{2720}{28\overline{)76160}}$$

Step 1:  2720 (the answer)   2 + 7 + 2 + 0 + 11; 11 - 9(1x9) = <u>2</u>
Step 2:  28 (the divisor)   2 + 8 = 10; 10 - 9(1x9) = <u>1</u>
Step 3:  Multiply 2 x 1 = 2
Step 4:  76160 (the dividend)  7 + 6 + 1 +6 + 0 = 20; 20 -18 (2x9) = <u>2</u>
Step 5:  The answer in Step 3 must equal the answer in Step 4: 2 = 2

**In cases of answers with remainders, the steps are slightly different.**

$$\frac{16\ R\ 3}{15\overline{)243}}$$

Step 1:  16 R 3 (the answer) 1 + 6 = <u>7</u>. *Ignore the remainder for now.*
Step 2:  15 (the divisor): 1 + 5 = <u>6</u>
Step 3:  Mulitply 7 x 6 = 42. NOW add the remainder. 42 + 3 = 45.
          45 - 45 (5 x 9) = <u>0</u>
Step 4:  243 (the dividend)  2 + 4 + 3 = 9; 9 - 9 (1x9) = 0
Step 5:  The answer to Step 3 must equal the answer to Step 4. 0 = 0

# Fractions

With a lot of persistence and effort, Kurt learned the basic math skills. He would take quizzes as we worked to make sure he was remembering everything he had learned. He did so well that we moved on to fractions.

First we discussed what fractions stand for. "Kurt," I explained, "the bottom number, the denominator, tells the total number of parts the whole unit is divided into. The top number of the fraction, the numerator, states how many parts of the whole or unit are needed." I showed him two examples:

# Tutoring Math

1. There are three trees on Mary's worksheet. She has to color two of them with leaves and write in fraction form how many of the trees have leaves.

Mary wrote 2/3.

2. Jim's drawing requires 5/6 of a sheet of paper. First he has to divide and mark the whole sheet into 6 equal parts.

He counts out five of the six parts and then cuts the paper. Now he has the exact size he needs.

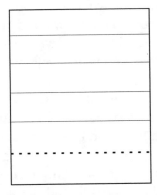

Kurt understood these simple fractions.

Learning the differences in fractions is not easy. Pictures in a book are okay, but Kirk couldn't move or manipulate them to show differences. So we used measuring cups, a set that included cups that measured 1/4, 1/3, 1/2, 3/4 and one whole cup. We also used food coloring to color 1/2 cup of water green, 1/4 cup blue, 1/3 cup yellow, and the whole cup red. Then having found several clear 8 ounce glasses, Kurt poured the colored water from the measuring cups into the clear colored glasses. Now he could clearly see the differences in the fractional amounts. And then he moved on to equivalent fractions.

Kurt then took three equal rectangles, cut one into thirds, one into halves, and left the third as it was. He had to use two of the thirds and one of the halves and try to cover the uncut rectangle completely and perfectly. He twisted and turned the cut out pieces but soon saw that they would not fit on the card. He looked contemplatively at the pieces. "There must be a way to add halves and thirds," he mused. "It must be possible, but how?" And so he learned about equivalent fractions and common denominators.

Kurt was beginning to think mathematically. I explained improper fractions using the measuring cups again. If Kurt added 1/2 cup of water to 3/4 cups of water, he had more than the one whole cup could hold.

Manipulating pieces of paper, water in measuring cups, buttons, or other objects is a sure way to teach kids. They can feel, see, and move things in a way that makes learning more comprehensible.

As Kurt mastered fractions, his confidence grew. We cut back from two sessions a week to one. And then the day came when Kurt felt he would like to try doing his work on his own. I agreed, gave him my "blessings" and said, "I doubt that you will ever need me, but just in case, don't ever be ashamed or embarrassed to call. I'll always be here if you need me." I must admit I had ambivalent feelings about Kurt's leaving. I had learned a lot about him in the months that he had been coming to me. As his confidence grew, so did his personality. He was funny, warm and a joy to work with. But it was time for him to go and we both knew it.

I have a rule I live by. I don't want my students to stay with me forever. I want them to be able to go to school and do their work without my help. As soon as the students and I feel they have mastered their skills, it's time to go on without me. So we work hard but as quickly as we can to attain that goal. My students and their parents appreciate this and provide many references.

## Calculators

Of course the easiest way to do math and to check it is to use calculators. There is one enormous problem with that. Kids don't learn how to do math by themselves. Students come to classes and when they have to add numbers as small as 9 + 6, they turn to their calculators. They use them for everything.

When calculators worked with batteries, it was easy to tell students that they had better learn to do the basics themselves. What if their batteries went dead in the middle of exams or when they were adding up the prices of everything they bought when they went shopping?

Calculators are now solar operated so there is no problem. But calculators are so much a part of life, it almost feels as if the world cannot run without them. At least at lot of students must feel that way.

There are teachers who refuse to let elementary school children use calculators. They must learn to do the math by themselves. These teachers deserve praise. They are making students think instead of acting like robots.

There are a great many other teachers who tell their students that it's all right to bring calculators to class and use them. That is fine if kids are learning higher math concepts such as trigonometry, logarithms, and calculus or are in classes like bookkeeping or accounting.

Calculators have their places. But not in math classes when kids are learning basics.

## Teaching Math Concepts: Addition

Math problems occur at every level. Imagine a five or six-year-old who can count to 10 but cannot understand that any whole number plus one is the next larger counting number. Ask a very small tot his age, and he will hold up 2 fingers or 3 or 4; he knows that holding up an added finger each year makes him older. But that doesn't teach him 2 plus 1 is 3, or 3 plus 1 is 4. A child has to be taught the ideas of numbers and counting things — two feet, one nose, 10 fingers. Again I always use concrete examples, anything I can group together or separate.

Buttons are great for children of primary school age. They come in all sizes, shapes and very bright colors - and kids love bright colors! When you teach addition, give your students 6 buttons and ask how many ways they can get 6 using 2 piles of buttons. Eventually they'll see that piles of 5 and 1, 4 and 2, and 3 and 3 all add up to 6.

If your students are having real problems with addition and subtraction, maybe they're having difficulty learning what counting numbers really stand for. Take an object like an egg carton and label the cups from one to 12. Have your students place one object in the #1 cup, 2 in the cup with #2, etc. Change the kinds of counting objects frequently so that they won't lose interest too quickly.

## Math Terms

Terms are confusing to many students. For younger students, a few of these terms are:

1. Jim has 3 books; Mary has 4. How many do they have *altogether*?
2. Joe has 6 books; Amy has 3. *How many more* does Joe have?
3. What is the *difference* between 5 and 7?
4. Jack has 5 cookies. Jill has 3. *How many less* does Jill have?

And for the older students:

1. "*Of*" which means to multiply (20% of 80 = ?)
2. "*Out of*" which means to divide (What % is 5 out of 4?)

3. In the equation, *"x is 5 less than 3x,"* "is" means "equals" and "5 less than 3x" means 3x minus 5. If students have trouble understanding this, give them easy examples such as 2 less than 6 means 6 - 2.

Be sure to determine which terms the kids don't know; once they learn them, math becomes much easier.

## Games for Teaching

When your young students are ready to learn to add and subtract, there are many games you can make that will teach them and still keep them interested. Make sure to include yourself as one of the players. Have a pair of dice ready and then make two sets of 13 cards, each having a number from 0 to 12, and place them face up in a row like this:

**0 1 2 3 4 5 6 7 8 9 10 11 12**

Dice with eight sides are great but may be hard to find. If you can locate them, you can use cards up to 16. Take turns with your student rolling dice and then either subtract the two numbers shown or add them together. If the sum or difference is the same as one of the numbers on the face-up cards, turn that card face down. For example, if the dice thrown show 6 and 4, the player can either add 6 and 4 and turn over 10 or subtract 4 from 6 and turn over the 2. The first person to turn over all his cards wins.

Remember, you can also use 2 dice to multiply up to 36. With 8-sided dice, you can multiply to 64. You will need two sets of cards for each multiplication answer, one for your students and one for you.

Working with dice is extremely useful for those students who have trouble understanding what numbers stand for. They see the dots and as they count them, they connect the fact that 4 dots on a die is another way of showing the number 4.

When I first started tutoring, I made many large, empty bingo cards with 25 squares, five by five, and I made my own bingo games, depending on what the child was learning. Some cards were designed for addition and subtraction through 10, others through 19. For multiplication, some cards had the 2's and 3's tables, some had 3's, 4's, and 5's tables, and others had 5's and 6's and 7's, and so on. The problems were on index cards and the students really had to know the answer before they could cover the number on the bingo card. To make it even more fun, I took an 8x10 poster card for each of my students and drew a line down the middle of the card with their names on one side of the card and mine on the other. Whoever won the games could paste a star vertically in their column. When the students' columns were completed, they won a prize and started on a new poster. I made a colorful bulletin board to pin the posters on, and the children loved it! *And they learned!*

To this day, what amazes me is that they won the games most of the time. I never cheated for them unless they said, "I really want to win this game." I'd look them straight in the eye and say, "You really want to win this game? No matter how?" And if they said yes, I would let them win. We were aware that I was sometimes cheating, but it was out in the open, so it didn't matter.

Don't be discouraged if your students seem to be taking a very long time to learn. Younger students sometimes can only learn one subject at a time, but they are *subconsciously* absorbing what you are teaching them. Then one day, everything falls into place and they understand and are able to learn all the concepts you have been working on.

## Building Self Confidence

Some students are anxious and make learning very difficult for themselves. They need to build their self-confidence.

When they do, their anxiety disappears and they are able to learn the material much more easily.

Abby, 10 years old, skipped into my office, her ponytail bobbing up and down. She glanced around the room as she settled into a chair. "Hi," she announced in a carefree voice. "I'm Abby. Do you know that I'm here cause I'm having trouble multiplying and dividing?"

I nodded.

"Okay," she laughed. "I can learn that!"

Abby was covering up her anxieties by pushing her inabilities to the back of her mind.

Abby was having more than a little trouble doing her math problems. Actually, she had no idea where to start. So we began at the beginning. As we worked on her homework, we were also working on why numbers worked as they did. Why did 2 piles of 4 buttons equal 8 buttons altogether? Why did a pile of 8 buttons separated into 2 piles always have 4 buttons in each pile? Several weeks went by, and Abby was showing great improvement and feeling very proud of herself. Then one day, she sat down at our table, her ponytail drooping over her bent head. "I failed my work today," she whispered and then was quiet. She unfolded a very crumpled ditto sheet and handed it to me.

## Word Problems!

The one type of math I hadn't asked her about before. I quickly scanned the paper. One of the problems said:

> "Jane and June went to the store. Jane bought 5 pencils. June bought 4 more than Jane. How many pencils did the girls buy altogether?"

Abby was lost. What was she supposed to do? It didn't take long to discover that Abby didn't know what the word problems were stating, what they were asking for, and most of all, she didn't know whether to subtract, multiply or divide.

So we worked on the meanings of word problems. If she was asked the *difference* between items, she subtracted. If the question was how many items did people have *altogether*, the word *altogether* meant to add.

Another of Abby's problems read:

Mary bought 10 pounds of sugar. She wanted to put 2 pounds of sugar into separate bags. How many bags did she need?

Abby could not picture what to do with the 10 pounds of sugar or the bags. Until she could see that the 10 pound bag had to be divided into smaller amounts to be put into the two pound bags, we could not proceed. I changed the problem. "What if we had 10 teaspoons of sugar in a bowl and we wanted to put two teaspoons in each cup? How many cups would we need?" When she still look puzzled, I put ten teaspoons of sugar into a bowl and several empty cups on the table. Abby then put two teaspoons of sugar in a cup, subtracting those two from ten. She repeated this step and subtracted two from eight, then two from six, two from four, two from two until the bowl was empty. Looking at what she had done, she learned that she had used five cups; therefore, there are five twos in ten, and ten divided by two is five. The answer to this problem is accomplished by division.

Word problems are the source of a lot of the difficulties students have in math, no matter what their ages or grades, or what they are learning: percentages, ratios, algebra, geometry, etc. Many students are very bright, but for some reason, they have trouble sorting out the facts stated in the problem and what they are asked to do.

When my students have trouble with word problems, they learn that they must first read the entire problem in order to understand what they are being asked to find. Then they can start working, reading one phrase or sentence at a time and doing what is asked of them.

Not only elementary school students have trouble with word problems. High school students do too. For example:

Jane had a jar of cookies. She took out 5/6 of them. Her younger brother, Barry, reached into the jar and ate 2/3 of the cookies that were left. He ate 6 cookies. How many cookies were there originally?

Many students read only the first two sentences and immediately write down 5/6x. They don't realize if Jane removed 5/6 of the cookies, 1/6 of them were left. And then they don't read far enough to see Barry ate 2/3 of the cookies that were left. They do know "x" stands for the original number of cookies. And then they're stymied. So they reread the problem, and then go over the problem step by step, sentence by sentence. Barry took 2/3 of 1/6x, the amount left in the jar. And the number of cookies he ate equaled 6. Once they understand what is asked for, $2/3 (1/6\ x) = 1/9\ x = 6$, they do the problem easily and find the original number, 54.

Kids love games, especially ones you create yourself. When you develop new ones, you will find that every time you work out one new game or idea, you'll think of two others as good or better. It's really fun to see how many different ways you can think of to make learning more interesting and enjoyable. Abby didn't catch on immediately, but playing with different math games made word stories easier and more clear to her.

## Language of Math

Language plays a very big part in every kind of math. Look at algebra. It really has a language of its own! Variables, unknowns, absolute values, domains, etc. Do your students understand the terminology? Do they understand the symbols? Do they know that in math, as in English, we communicate by writing sentences? If we see $7t - 1 = 12$, we are reading the language of mathematics. Students must learn to translate those English phrases into mathematical ones so that problems can be solved, phrases such as "a number subtracted from 3 times another number" (in math terms this is 3n - y), "the sum of twice a number plus 15 is (2n + 15)" and "12 less than a number plus 6 is (n + 6) - 12)."

It also helps to know when your students started to have trouble in algebra. If they have been confused since the beginning of the term, you must retrace all the steps and start at the beginning of the book and work forward. If it is just in recent weeks or days that difficulties began, you need only go back to that point.

Can anyone tutor math? Some people think so. But in reality, a math tutor must have, or develop, three attributes:

1. knowing the math concepts that have to be taught,
2. having the ability to teach a problem in several different ways, and
3. understanding that the students you are seeing are frustrated and need your caring.

Having a text is a great help, and if you can get a teachers' edition, you'll have all the answers at hand. In geometry and algebra books, you'll often find the work itself.

Make sure your students do their problems in front of you so that you can catch their errors or where they are getting bogged down. Do not let students do two or three problems and then say, "Oh, I understand now. Let's move on." Too often they only understand for the moment and by the time they have returned home, they have forgotten what they have learned. Make absolutely sure that they understand thoroughly what you are working on even if it means practicing the same type of problem over and over again.

Work some of the problems with them, and then give only a little help on the next ones. And finally, ask them to do some of the problems by themselves. After all, when they go to school, you won't be there to help them with quizzes and tests.

## Fears About Math

Much of the difficulty in math stems from the fears that students have working with numbers. They develop anxieties at an early age, and it shows in their school work as soon as math becomes a little more complicated. Some of them may have heard their parents say, "I was never good in math. My child probably takes after me." Unfortunately kids then think math isn't important and so don't work very hard at it.

Watch for this and be understanding. Praise your students constantly. Even though they still may be making mistakes, give them praise. Say "That's great! Look at how well you're doing. You're terrific!"

With that kind of encouragement, there's nothing students can do but try to succeed. And most often, they will.

## Chapter Five

# Kids Who Puzzle Teachers: The Mislabeled Children

"Help! They want to retain my child!" Did you ever hear a sound that was at once a plaintive, but angry, cry? The female voice on the phone expressed both emotions. The woman related what was happening to her son.

"We're planning a beautiful summer. Vacation is about to begin, and Rick's teacher just dropped a bombshell! She wants Rick to repeat first grade. She says that he is very social and gets along well with his peers, and he listens to her and doesn't cause any problems. But he is way behind in reading and math. He knows his letters but cannot read words. He knows numbers but cannot add. And not only does she want him to repeat first grade, but she wants to put him into a learning disabilities class in the fall.

"Now I know that he's very bright. He reads words on store windows and on packages and he remembers everything. He's really funny and loves to imitate people on TV. You should see him. He keeps everyone in stitches!

"I don't want him kept back and I'll do anything to help him. Can you work with him this summer? I'll bring him as often as you think necessary. What do you think?"

This was not the first time I had heard about retaining children in first grade, nor the first time I had worked with them. I told Rick's mother not to let the school fail her son. "The emotional trauma of seeing all of your schoolmates continue on to second or third grade while you stay behind is really devastating. Occasionally there is a teacher who thinks the kids are too young to care or notice, but they do."

# The Mislabeled Children

I told her that maybe Rick was one of those youngsters who matures a little later and catches up during second grade. We talked a little longer and set up an appointment.

When Rick came, I met a good-looking boy with a big grin and sparkling eyes. He was wearing a large baseball hat and a jersey with the White Sox logo on it. After he became comfortable with me, I opened a workbook for beginning readers. I found that he knew many words. Granted, not as many as his classmates had learned, but enough for us to start with. As we worked, Rick asked questions — lots of them. And the questions were intelligent.

He worked with primary readers and the accompanying workbooks. He loved to draw so when he had to draw a line to the correct answer, he made the line into a plane. He sometimes made circles into squirrels or other animals. I went along with this unless it interfered with what we were trying to do. We played Bingo and my version of Scrabble. He could use two letter words when he was beginning to read. Rick came for tutoring three times a week during the summer, except for the two weeks when he was on vacation. By the end of the summer he was reading and doing very well. We had progressed from first primary readers to those that most classes were using at the end of first grade. We had concentrated on reading because I believed it was better to work on one subject, learn to do it well, and then move to another.

Rick's parents were thrilled with his learning. And then school started! I went to a meeting with his new teacher, old teacher, the learning disabilities teacher, the psychologist, and the principal. They had reviewed his work, they said, and felt that they could now take over in reading. It was better for Rick, they said, to be put in a LD class for reading. Therefore, would I please not work with him on reading anymore but concentrate only on math? I agreed. But I knew that from time to time I would ask Rick to read to me so I could see how he was doing.

In October, Rick's parents called. They were going on a three-week vacation and Rick's grandmother, who couldn't drive, was staying home with the children. "So, we have decided to stop the tutoring and let the teachers at school work with him. He is doing OK, so we feel we should try this."

Six weeks later, in the middle of November, I received a frantic call. It was Rick's mother. "We just came from the parent-teacher conference," she said. "Rick is having trouble with his letters again! Can you believe that? And all he does in school is work on simple vowel sounds. He's hardly even reading. My husband is furious! Tomorrow he is going to take Rick out of that LD class for good! Can you take Rick back again?" After agreeing, I asked permission to call his teacher. When I reached her, his teacher said that except for reading and math, Rick did well in class. He listened and took part in discussions. He was *fairly* confident but *very* social and outgoing.

I decided to gain whatever insight I could from Rick himself. He read for me. I checked his comprehension and vocabulary. He had fallen behind since school began, but I chalked that up to not having his reading reinforced in school. It is hard to teach 25 kids and give any amount of time to one youngster. Even in LD classes, there are sometimes a few children at a time and so a child doesn't get the individual attention he gets from a tutor. Rick and I quickly reviewed all the work we had done together and then proceeded once more.

We worked together twice a week, except for vacations, and by June, Rick had caught up with his class in reading and math. He was in the average group and doing well. His parents and I decided to let him have the summer free. If there were any problems in the fall, they would bring him back for a brush-up. Suffice to say, he didn't return that year. Three years later in fifth grade, Rick came back for help in math. Long division was an enigma. But now he had such self-confidence that in a matter of weeks, he understood the concepts and the steps in division and was able to take that knowledge back to the classroom. In other words, he was successful in a very short time.

There are often good reasons for students to be put in special classes, but in some cases children are placed there for wrong reasons. Sometimes kids are put into these classes because of poor work on a test. Kids can be so anxious during a test that they freeze and do poorly. Sometimes, because a child matures a little more slowly, his teacher thinks he needs LD or Special-Ed. Sometimes a teacher gets so frustrated trying to teach a certain child that he recommends a special class, believing that the child will get more individual help. These students really need to be in regular classes, getting a little extra help from their teachers, teachers' aides, volunteer teachers or with an outside professional tutor.

Larry was in third grade when his mother called me in October. He was in a special education class and doing very poorly. He hated school except for play time and recess. He was one of those kids who was sent to a school outside of his school district. He had no one from his class to play with after school. He couldn't read, his mother said, and couldn't do math either. She was very upset and confused because she had thought in a Special-Ed class, he would get special help and learn these skills. She wanted to bring Larry five times a week because she wanted him to get as much help as possible. I talked her into three times, saying that Larry needed time to play and have fun after school and that we should not make the idea of school such drudgery that he wouldn't respond to me or anyone.

Larry was a good looking boy who had had problems at home when he was just a tot. Since then, his mother had remarried, his new father had adopted him, and he had a baby step-brother. Larry lived in a beautiful home and had every material thing he needed and more.

When Larry arrived at my office, he, like many of the other kids do when they first meet me, had to feel things out. Would I "lose my cool" if he pushed books aside or if he scribbled on his papers? And what if he just wanted to talk and not listen? He tried every maneuver he could to test me and found that I remained calm. Before he left, I asked him how *he* felt about my visiting *his* classroom. I wondered if he would be embarrassed if the kids saw someone in the schoolroom talking about him. My gut reaction to his, "Sure, come if you want to," was that he really didn't think I would take the time nor care enough to make a special trip.

I called his teacher and received permission to visit. When I arrived, the kids were just coming in from gym. They were flushed and excited. The teacher and her aide tried to settle the children down, but couldn't. The aide started to erase the blackboards while the teacher came over to me. Most of the kids ran around the room, hid behind desks, and generally kept the rest of the class in a state of confusion. Larry finally noticed me and smiled incredulously. The aide finally was able to settle the kids down somewhat while Larry's teacher and I talked.

"He is too overstimulated," she reported. "He can't settle down to learn," she said. He had many emotional problems; he didn't get along with other children; he didn't listen and he didn't cooperate. But she was trying very hard with him and believed he would be able to read at the second grade level at the end of the year (at which time he would be going into her fourth grade Special-Ed class).

She gave me a copy of the materials she was using and asked that I follow her curriculum. I was also free to call and visit at any time. With that, she turned back to her still unruly class.

Larry had been learning the long vowel sounds first, but seemed to be having a lot of trouble with them. I decided to work with short vowels and see if, in his case, that might be better. It was.

Three times a week, an hour at a time, Larry came for lessons. There were many times that he didn't want to work. Instead, he talked about his new clothes or his toys. He told me about his weekend skiing trips with his family. He talked about his baby brother. He talked about anything in order not to have to do his lessons.

"My friends are mean," he complained. "They won't play with me very much. And, oh, how I hate school!"

Much of the time he was frustrated and would say, "I don't want to do this, let's play." Or, "I can't do this, let's do something else." In order to ease his frustrations, we'd play a learning game that he enjoyed and then return to the lessons. I'm sure he knew deep down that at 10 years old he didn't belong in a third grade where all he learned were simple addition and subtraction and all he read were first readers. Quite often he would say that he really wanted to be in a regular classroom and not with a "dummy" group. I used that wish to improve his attitude toward learning and to build his self-confidence.

Slowly, slowly Larry learned to read. In November, when we first started, he had been using a first reader. By February he had progressed to a second reader. As we worked, I began to wonder why Larry had been placed in a Special-Ed class to begin with. I asked his mother if she could get a copy of the original papers she signed. She did, and I was dumbfounded to see that there had been no legitimate excuse for placing Larry in a Special-Ed class. The papers did not refer to any emotional problem or real learning problems. His original second grade teacher had written that he was a slow learner and that he was taking too much of her time during reading classes. Larry, she wrote, had transferred from another area and was behind the class.

Larry's mother repeated what the teacher had said. "With all the extra help in Special-Ed classes, I am sure that Larry will advance quickly and return to a regular class by the end of the year." Eager for Larry to get the proper help, his mother signed the papers without checking into the class itself, the teacher who ran it, or the rules and regulations of the Special-Ed department. She trusted blindly and made a big mistake!

At the end of March, Larry and I were mid-way through the second reader. Larry could now add and subtract, regrouping when necessary. He was concentrating more and for longer periods of time.

I asked for a meeting with his teacher again. I felt that at the rate he was learning, maybe he could be mainstreamed into a slow third grade reading or math group. His teacher gave an emphatic and resounding "No!" "But," she said, "we'll think seriously about some kind of mainstreaming in fall. If he continues at this rate, we will mainstream him into a lower fourth grade math or reading class."

With this possibility, Larry tried even harder. When summer came, we changed his schedule to two hours a day, three times a week. And he worked!

Fall came, school started and Larry went to school, and found himself in the same Special-Ed class for every subject. Although he read well enough to be in a third grade reader and he was doing simple multiplication, the teacher felt he should be kept where he was. I went to another meeting. This time his teacher gave me a set of goals with a promise that Larry would be moved if and when he met these goals. Once again, we went to work.

In November, I believed we had met his teacher's goals, but she didn't agree to mainstreaming him except for music and art. Needless to say, his parents were upset, and so was Larry. He felt he was working for nothing, and he was losing any self-confidence he had gained. Every day, I told him that he must keep working. We were going to beat this thing!

# The Mislabeled Children

In January, his parents informed me that they were moving into a new school district the following fall, and they asked me to visit the principal there.

I did and met a delightful man whose students are very important to him. I told him Larry's story, and he agreed that Larry might be in the wrong class. His school had classes for kids at all levels of every grade, whether average, above average, slow or gifted. He told me what was expected in June of their very lowest fourth grade class and asked if I could help Larry achieve those skills by then. If so, the school psychologists and the teachers, as well as he himself, would take a good look at Larry and see what they felt could be done.

I told Larry the possibility of being in a regular 5th grade class in the fall. He was ecstatic! We both felt that *this time* a goal was in sight and attainable. At the end of May, I went to a meeting with all the school officials in his new school, and made an impassioned speech (I wish I had been a little less emotional.) Unfortunately, I had to leave early for my next student. Much later, Larry and his mother burst into my office. "Larry, tell Mrs. Shapiro what happened!"

"I'm going to be in fifth grade!" he beamed. "I really am!" He looked brighter and happier, and I felt 10 feet tall!

☆ ☆ ☆

Rick and Larry were almost among the "lost" kids in our schoolrooms. They might have ended up hating school so much that they ultimately would lose out on their educations. Poor diagnosis and lack of insight into the "whole" child can be very detrimental.

This situation happens more often than anyone would care to admit. If parents come to you troubled about the label a school is putting on their children and have some doubts about it, listen to them. See if you can find a way to help their children without holding them back, without putting them in special education classes or in special schools. There is a real difference between children who are truly learning-disabled and those who are just a little slower in learning.

## Chapter Six

# The Special "Special" Children: Special Ed

I heard the outer door to my waiting room open and close quietly. I was expecting a new student, a high school sophomore who was in Special-Ed classes. The sound of muffled voices filtered through my office door as I continued working with the student by my side. Suddenly the quiet was broken by shrill, loud voices. I could hear angry words pouring out, and I found myself unable to concentrate. I excused myself and went to the door. Sitting in the waiting room were an attractive dark-haired woman and a slightly disheveled, but pretty, teenager. I introduced myself and met Kim, who appeared to be extremely frustrated and agitated, and her mother, cool and efficient, who was trying to reason with her daughter.

"We're disturbing Mrs. Shapiro," she said. "We'll discuss this at home."

Kim was not in a receptive mood. I came over to her and said quietly, "Kim, I'm sorry you have to wait a few minutes. I will be with you as soon as possible and then we can talk as long as you'd like."

This seemed to satisfy her and I went back to my desk. While I continued teaching, my mind wandered. "What did I get myself into this time?" I wondered. "I hope my patience level is at an all time high. I'll sure need it!" And those were some of the truest words I'd ever thought.

## Characteristics of These Students

The one characteristic that describes all special education students, no matter how old they are, is a high frustration level. If they are upset with school or events at home, they'll show those feelings. If they are unable to grasp what you are teaching them, they may shout or jump up from their chairs and walk away. The older students will often cry, "I can't do it!" or "You're making me crazy!" The younger students mutter, "This is boring. Let's do something else."

Their attention span is extremely short. You can be teaching them to multiply, and suddenly, they'll ask, "Did I tell you about the snakes I have at home?" Their minds wander, and they have trouble staying on one subject.

These kids know they're different. They know they're different by the classes they're in. They know they've been labeled "Special-Ed" and to them that means "dumb" or "mental" or whatever the jargon happens to be at the time. Students their own age don't want to play with them, and they feel pretty much out of the stream of things. School work is hard for them, and so they try to avoid doing any lessons.

## Building Rapport

So how do you teach them? First, you must become their friend, one who really cares *for* them and *about* them.

You must make them understand that they can talk about anything they want, their frustrations, their anger, their hopes and dreams. And if you let them spill their anger, you must also be very, very sure that they know you will not repeat to anyone else something that they want you to keep secret. They need to know they can trust you, and that you are, indeed, a trusting and caring friend. Being that kind of friend means, however, that there may be times when you hear some very important information that you feel a parent should know. If so, tell your student how you feel and why, and ask if you may talk to their parents. Most of the time, the reply will be "Okay, go ahead." These kids often want to tell their parents themselves, but they are afraid. They think that you will somehow protect them from what they expect will be their parents' anger or misunderstanding.

The students also want to like you as a teacher. Will you tolerate any distractions that they may make? Will you let them change the subject and digress occasionally? What if they do talk about snakes or their dad's new power rake? What if they can't sit still and want to wander around the room?

A good tutor goes with the "flow." If a student wants to tell you about his snakes, listen. I sure learned a lot about reptiles one year. (I still hate them!) Talk about their world, their hockey games or parties. The proper time for such conversation during a tutoring session differs with the age of the student. Students who have reached the 6th grade level can be told that you have "free periods" at the beginning and end of your sessions. If you find that their attention span is too short to last until the end of the period, take a few minutes in the middle for a break. If the students are very young, tell them gently you will talk as soon as you finish what you are doing. Pull them back firmly but warmly, and they will do as you say.

## Phrases They Use About Schoolwork

If the younger students say they are "bored" or the work itself is "boring," it may mean they don't understand it. They may say that out of habit. They become so used to saying something is "boring," whether or not they are able to do the work, that it really has no meaning. "That word is a cop-out," I tell my students. "You use it so that you won't have to work. So from now on, you can't use that word here with me." And you know what? After I say that, they stop using the word!

## Scheduling

I try to see Special-Ed kids at least twice a week. And if I do, I sometimes strike a bargain with them. "On the first day of the week," we agree, "I will teach the subjects the way I feel is best and on the second visit, you can choose the books or games we'll use. But, it must be within the boundaries I make." The kids love this arrangement because they feel they have some say in their learning. And that is good for them because in school, they are *never* in command. They are told what they must do at all times.

## Building Self Confidence

The main idea in working with these children is to build their self-confidence. (I must say "You *can* do it," at least 20 times each session.) You must impress upon them that one day they will want to leave home, and they will have to be able to handle money, work, and socialize with all types of people. If they don't learn these skills now, who will do it for them?

I have a 12-year-old student who is just now learning short and long vowel sounds though he knows many sight words. It took a whole summer for him to learn the short sounds and retain them, but now he can read more easily, and he is very proud of himself.

Although he still has trouble in school, his teachers do not spend enough individual time with him. He has to do most of the work on his own and most of his reading silently, so who hears his mistakes? Therefore, it is even more important to get much praise from his tutor so that he will continue to learn, albeit slowly.

Teaching Special-Ed students is similar to teaching any slow student. As I've said before, it just takes a lot more time and a lot more patience. What you can teach an average child in weeks may take months with a Special-Ed student. You must realize at the outset that if a child is truly a Special-Ed student, he may never read better than the 4th grade level, and he may never do math beyond the basics. Once that is understood, you can teach the student what he must know to deal with the world after he leaves school.

## Teaching About Money

I have discovered that many Special-Ed students reach high-school without any idea of how to handle money. They have never gone shopping alone; they don't know how to figure out actual amounts of paper money and/or coins to use for items they want to purchase or the amount of money due them if there is change to be made. In school they may have been shown pictures of money and then told to add or subtract in story problems, but the work was so abstract that they could not make the transfer to real money situations. So I developed a method of teaching them how to use money. On my desk I keep a jar of change (about $5.00 in silver coins and pennies). The first thing I teach them is that a nickel is worth 5 cents, a dime is worth 10 cents, a quarter is 25 cents and so on. The average person will count to 37 cents quickly, knowing the value of coins. Can you imagine how these kids do it? Some use all nickels because they know the 5's tables. "5, 10, 15, 20, 25, 30, 35," and then they'll see the need for 2 pennies. "36, 37!" And they are so proud. Some students use dimes because they know the 10's tables. "10, 20, 30," then they are stymied. How do they get to 37 cents? Some will use 7 pennies, some will remember that a nickel is 5 cents and because they know both 5's and 10's tables, they figure out that they can say 30, 35 and then add the two pennies.

You will find that starting with a quarter is hard for these kids. If they add a dime to that amount, they find it hard to visualize how much money they have altogether, because there is no table that says 25, then 35. Adding 5, on the other hand, is easy because those numbers are in the 5's table, 25, 30, 35.

I must repeat, it is very important that these students know the value of each coin. Too many of us take that knowledge for granted, but these kids really don't understand that a dime and 10 cents are the same thing.

Once they have mastered these facts, I begin asking questions. "How many pennies are in a nickel? And how many pennies and/or nickels are in a dime? What is a nickel worth? And how much is a dime worth? How many ways can I make change that adds up to a dime? 10 pennies? 5 pennies and a nickel? 2 nickels? A dime?"

I do the same with a quarter, a half dollar and a dollar. This whole process takes a lot of patience. For Kim, patience was in short supply.

"I can't," she cried out in frustration and with one swish of her hand, swept the coins off the table. They flew all over the floor. And then Kim cried miserably.

"It's okay," I said. "This is hard stuff. It takes a lot of time." I waited, holding my breath to see if Kim would accept that and then I suggested, "Let's pick up the coins. We can do other things now, and if you feel like it later, we can try this again."

She stopped crying, wiped her eyes with the backs of her hands, and we began picking up the coins. I kept reassuring her quietly: everything was fine, no problem. Kim put the coins back into the jar with a look that showed me that we would not work on money again that day!

The next time we met, she tentatively tipped the jar over and we renewed the lessons with the coins.

Once my students master these "simple" lessons (and with some of my students that takes months!) we begin the more difficult work.

In school, the kids are told they must use the least number of coins possible. I don't know why this is so important. It may be because many books concentrate on how few coins can be used to reach a certain amount of money. For a total of 39 cents, the students are expected to come up with one quarter, one dime and four pennies. (6 coins altogether.)

But some students don't comprehend what the least amount of coins should be. They may try the quarter all right. But then they'll use *two nickels* instead of the dime plus 4 pennies (which makes 7 coins.) Or they'll use 3 dimes, 1 nickel, and 4 pennies (8 coins.)

And then the teacher will say, in a loud, impatient voice, "No, do it again!"

And the kids become frustrated. They know they've counted out 39 cents, but they don't understand what they've done wrong.

I feel that I, as a tutor, have the responsibility of removing some of that frustration. So I try the positive approach. I say, "Hey, that's good! Do you think there's another way we can get 39 cents, too? With even fewer coins?"

And with a smile, they will try again.

I try to make it clear that there usually is more than one "right" way to make change, and it's to their advantage to know this.

I never say, "No," and the only time I say, "Try again," is if they count out the wrong amount of change.

I also teach the kids to figure out what their change will be if they give $1.00 to a clerk and the item is only 52 cents.

There are two methods to count change. One is counting from the cost, 52 cents, up to a dollar. The other is to subtract (in your head) 52 cents from $1.00, learning that 48 cents is the exact change required and then counting out that amount of change. The latter is done in two steps, so I don't dwell on that method with Special-Ed students.

I ask the kids to count out loud as they figure their change. That way I can hear if and when they make an error. I can hear them saying, "53, 54, 55" as they use the pennies, and then "65, 75," as they add two dimes, and finally, "$1.00," as they add the quarter. I don't care how they make the change as long as they understand what they are doing...and they get the right amount of change counted out.

I even give my students homework so that they can work with money between sessions. I draw charts on which I list amounts of change that they must make with coins. They also have a jar of coins to work with at home. Then they list what they have used. The "A" chart is used to figure out amounts that they might need to buy something, and the "B" chart is for figuring out the amount of change they would get if they purchased an item and gave the clerk more than the actual cost. When they return for their next session, I check the charts.

| WHAT KIND OF CHANGE DO I NEED TO MAKE THE AMOUNTS OF MONEY SHOWN BELOW? | | | | |
|---|---|---|---|---|
| Amount | Quarter | Dimes | Nickels | Pennies |
| .83 | 3 | | 1 | 3 |
| .83 | 2 | 3 | | 3 |
| .17 | | | | |
| .68 | | | | |
| .42 | | | | |
| .59 | | | | |
| .74 | | | | |
| .52 | | | | |
| .36 | | | | |
| .24 | | | | |

**CHART "A"**

| WHAT KIND OF CHANGE WILL I GET FROM $1.00 IF I BUY SOMETHING FOR THE FOLLOWING AMOUNTS? | | | | | |
|---|---|---|---|---|---|
| Cost | Quarter | Dimes | Nickels | Pennies | Change |
| .39 | 2 | 1 | | 1 | .61 |
| .88 | | | | | |
| .27 | | | | | |
| .36 | | | | | |
| .56 | | | | | |
| .89 | | | | | |
| .44 | | | | | |
| .32 | | | | | |
| .66 | | | | | |
| .19 | | | | | |

**CHART "B"**

It's surprising how quickly the kids begin to learn when they practice at home daily. And how excited they become as they master the skills needed to work with money!

I do tell them there is no special way to make change, as long as they do it right. But, they are not allowed to use more than 4 pennies. If I allow them to use five or more pennies, they may not work with nickels and dimes as much as they should.

Kim, the student I mentioned at the beginning of this chapter, would come into my office, a very angry, frustrated 15-year-old. Within minutes, she'd begin to scream that she couldn't multiply 4 x 4, that no one understood how hard she was trying. Her brain just wasn't making the right connections. She would toss her papers away, stand up and stamp her feet, and pace up and down, all the time crying out in frustration. I'd sit quietly and wait.

When she was through, I'd ask her what she was *really* feeling. What I heard in response was her own feeling of inadequacy. She had to be able to talk about it with someone. She knew she couldn't raise her voice in school or throw things.

"No one listens to me. Nobody cares how I feel. And if I get mad — boy! they get madder! They don't see how hard I'm trying and they don't care. I don't understand them. What do they want from me?"

To make things worse for her, Kim had a speech impediment which often made it difficult for people to understand what she was saying, especially when she was upset. So her feelings came out in my office as she stamped her feet, raised her voice and tossed her papers away.

After many weeks, Kim began to tell me how she felt without losing control. When she couldn't do a problem or comprehend a paragraph, she would begin to get stirred up. I could actually see her starting to churn, and I would wait to see how she would handle her feelings. Most of the time she would glance at me and when she'd see me sitting there quietly, waiting for her to calm down, she'd give a self-conscious laugh, and say, "Okay, just a minute. I'll start all over again."

Kim could not multiply numbers beyond 4 x 4. If I asked her to multiply any larger numbers together, for example, 4 x 6, she would write 6 + 6 + 6 + 6 and add them together, using her fingers. We tried repeatedly to find a way for her to memorize the multiplication tables, but that seemed almost impossible. We settled for her learning to add and subtract fairly well and using a calculator when she needed to multiply or divide.

Because Kim read at about a fourth grade level, we worked hard on decoding and comprehension. She read aloud very poorly, skipping a word here and there, leaving off endings of words and mispronouncing many of them, I was always amazed at how well she understood *what* she read.

Kim was my student for three years. In the last two of those years, I didn't have a student who worked any harder than she.

In the middle of her junior year, she got a job in a fast-food restaurant doing the clean-up work and making french fries. The manager knew that although she could not handle money, she was a fine worker, and Kim basked in the knowledge that she was capable of handling a paying job. Up until then, she had been helping her parents in their respective offices, cleaning up and answering phones. But now she was on her own!

Kim was one of those students who knew nothing about money. She carried single dollar bills and trusted the world to be honest when she bought school supplies. If she went to a restaurant, she trusted waiters and waitresses to give her the right change.

As time went by and Kim continued on her job, her confidence grew and she felt she should learn about money. We began using the methods I've outlined and twice a week, we worked on making change or figuring costs. She concentrated totally and was very excited when she remembered from week to week how to deal with money. Eventually when someone had time to help Kim, the manager let her work the register for a short while.

Now when Kim came to my office, she was no longer disheveled. She was very conscious of her appearance. Her long, dark curly hair was combed and her clothes were the latest teen-age fashions.

Finally it was her senior year in high school. Kim had always wanted to work with children and now that was on her mind. "Mrs. Shapiro," she asked plaintively, "is there any way you can see that I can work in a nursery school or day-care center? I'd really like to be a teacher, but I know I can't make it in college."

Fortunately for Kim, the woman who was the head of the Special-Ed department at her high school knew of a college that accepted a small percentage of Special-Ed students. So Kim's parents wrote to the school and took her there to see the campus. She loved it. But would they accept her? I wish I could describe the joy in Kim's voice the evening she called me to tell me she had been accepted. And why was she accepted? Because they had heard about the amount of effort she had put into learning, and they felt she would continue to study hard at their school.

Kim entered college. I heard from her about once a week. She had her "ups and downs" trying to adjust to being away from the security of her home and family, but she did great and loved it.

Ann, another high-school Special-Ed student, was from a different school. She, too, had never learned about money. Would you believe a girl of 17 who had never been to a store to buy anything? Not even a candy bar or chewing gum? She had no idea of what a dime or a nickel meant. Ann started coming to me in November of her junior year. Because she read on a 6th grade level, we worked on reading comprehension, but, most of all, we concentrated on money problems. After four months, I asked her to go to the grocery store and buy dessert to take with her school lunch. She was terrified at the suggestion!

"I can't! I just can't! What if I don't have enough money? What if I count wrong? Please don't make me do that. Not yet."

I reassured her that whatever she bought would cost less than one dollar and she already knew how to count the right amounts of money to that dollar. We role-played: I was the checkout clerk and Ann practiced buying a cupcake or candy bar. Still very anxious, she reluctantly agreed to try this assignment.

She decided to buy a cupcake. She took a lot of coins, added up how much change she needed, and went up to the counter. The clerk put the money in the register, and gave

# The Special "Special" Children: Special Ed

Ann the bag with the cupcake. Ann bounced out to the car as if someone had given her the moon. When she told me the story, she had such a huge smile, I thought she'd burst!

Each week for four weeks, she bought one item, and then I complicated matters. "Ann," I said, "tomorrow buy two things for your lunch, like bread and cheese, or a soft drink and a dessert. I don't care what as long as there are two items." After Ann worked on that assignment for two weeks, I called her mother and asked her if she would give Ann a list of three or four things to buy at the store. By June, when Ann was out of school, she was beginning to help her mother with the grocery list. She didn't return the next fall. I hoped that I had helped her to deal with life outside of school.

☆  ☆  ☆

Up to now, I have been talking about Special-Ed students in high school, but I've also had many Special-Ed students in lower grades. Joe was a 12-year-old with whom I worked on vowel sounds. His class consisted of 12 children who ranged in age from 9 to 12 and who worked on second or third-grade levels. He was mainstreamed for music, art and gym classes with the regular sixth grade class, and although that sounds good on paper, it was very upsetting to Joe. The sixth graders knew he was from a special class and so ignored him most of the time. He had to travel to a certain school for Special-Ed by bus, and that ride took 45 minutes or more each way. He, therefore, did not see the children from his neighborhood until sometime after 4:00 in the afternoon.

Joe was feeling isolated and wanted to move to another school. His unhappiness showed in his work. His reading was sporadic. Sometimes he read at an early third grade level and sometimes he read much below that. In school, he read orally about two and a half hours a week and silently for close to three hours. He could not sound out many words phonetically unless someone was with him to make sure he remembered what the short or long vowel sounds sounded like. He had trouble with blends, like pl, str, ch, etc. Words with two or more syllables often threw him. He had been in Special-Ed classes for five or six years and he still needed help.

When Joe started seeing me, he would work for three or four minutes, complain that everything was boring, run to the door to make sure his mother was waiting for him, and then want to play games. His excuse for everything was, "How am I supposed to know that? You know I'm in special classes! You know I'm not smart!"

For Joe (like others) praise was vital. He had to know that he could learn, that he could read better. I knew that I had to build his self confidence. I found story books he could read easily while he worked on vowel sounds. Joe had never listened to himself while sounding out words so all of the short vowels sounded alike — *bit* was bet or bat, *top* was tip or tup. And cap and cape sounded alike. The two sounds of 'ea,' as in bead or bread, were impossible. We started working on sounds of all the vowels, short ones first and then the long ones. I gave him work to do at home with his parents and I asked him to read into a tape recorder.

Joe's handwriting looked like crow-tracks. It was almost impossible to read. He had learned to write by copying the letters the way he thought they were formed. He had never really had handwriting lessons. But I felt that I wanted to concentrate on his reading and comprehension.

That summer Joe played on a baseball team but found that a difficult sport. He went to soccer camp for a week but didn't find himself there either.

In the fall, Joe began to be very impatient about learning. Now, more than ever, he wanted to go to a school close to his home where he could be with his friends, and he wanted to be mainstreamed so he wouldn't feel so left out. His parents thought that he was not getting enough help in his class, that his work was too simple, and that he needed more individual time with his teacher. Everyone was frustrated.

My reaction was to say, "Joe, only you can make it possible to be mainstreamed. We, your parents and I, cannot go to school for you and do your work. You have to show your teachers how quietly you can sit and listen in class and how much effort you are willing to put forth. If you show them how hard you are working and how much you're improving in reading and math, then they will start thinking about moving you into regular classrooms. Just remember, *you* have to do it. We can show you how, but only you can do it."

This became my weekly sermon. It must have helped because, although the teachers were still loath to give him harder work, they did note that he was acting better in the classroom.

Meanwhile, I used many different workbooks. When I didn't find what I liked, I wrote my own. I wrote lessons using the words, "to, too, and two." I wrote lessons that taught "following directions." For example, I would draw six squares and draw a picture of a house in each one. Then under the pictures, on the bottom half of the page, were directions like these.

1. If the house in Picture One has a tree, add flowers.

2. Put curtains in the windows on Picture Four.

3. Find the empty window in Picture Six and add a plant.

Many of the kids would just go from picture to picture in sequential order without noting that there were particular directions for each square.

I also wrote stories which not only included comprehension but math as well. The stories were simple, but I kept them interesting, and I taught two subjects at once!

Joe started making progress. He had joined a hockey team and finally seemed to find his niche. He loved it and talked hockey as much as I let him. He was still upset about his classroom, but he had found something he could do and which he enjoyed.

He was not as socially adept as most 12 years old boys. One could tell that he was slower than his peers, but he was generally a happy boy and I knew he would manage to learn enough to live in our world.

## TO SUM UP: Tutoring Special-Education Children

1.   Be sure to be very patient with each of them. There will be days when nothing you do or say will settle them down. Give them space to let their frustrations out. That alone is a great help to them.

2.   Tutor them very slowly. Don't expect quick results. Go over lessons again and again, if necessary, and don't be discouraged if they forget much of it by the next session. They really are retaining *something* each visit.

3.   Forget how old they actually are and remember what they are able to learn. Teaching a 17-year-old how to use money seems ridiculous, but some students honestly know nothing about it.

4.   Listen to them. Be their friend as well as their tutor. They'll work harder if they know you care about them.

5.   PRAISE, PRAISE, PRAISE! There is nothing as important as telling them repeatedly how great they are and how well they are doing. Build their self-confidence and watch them blossom!

Chapter Seven

# Working With Homebound Kids

There are children who, because of serious injuries or debilitating illnesses, cannot go to school They must stay at home and have tutors come to them. Schools are responsible for the education of all children; they must send teachers to the student. For a nominal fee, they hire tutors, give them some instructions regarding the students' health and classwork, and then send them on their way.

It was a hot, muggy day in early August. I was sitting in the shade of our maple tree trying to catch a slight breeze and thinking about the plans we had just completed for a huge addition to our house. Part of it would be my office with a waiting room and its own outside door. I had just recently moved my offices from a nearby building back to the recreation room in my home until the addition was completed. The construction was to begin on September 1 and I was already losing my cool! Not from the heat and humidity and not from the costs or possible friction with the construction company. Oh, no! I was unnerved thinking about all the noises I was going to have to endure all day. How many ways, I mused, could I think of to get away from the house — at least until 3:00 when I started teaching. I thought of shopping — I'm not a shopper. I thought of going back to school to finish my graduate degree — I didn't feel like studying all night or writing papers. I kept searching for ideas.

Then early one Monday morning I heard the shrill sound of the phone bell. "No one calls me at this hour for tutoring," I muttered as I reached for the phone.

"Eileen?" a man's voice asked. "Hi. This is Jack Peters." Jack was the father of one of my students and a lawyer. For a moment I wondered if something was wrong. Then he continued. "Eileen, I was wondering if you would like to help me on a case I have. My client, Bill MacArthur, is a 14-year-old boy who was in an automobile accident last year. He was hospitalized for several more months and was supposed to see a tutor from his school until he came home. From what I understand, the tutor only came a few times. Mac is home, but the doctors say he can't go back to school for several months. So he needs a tutor to come to him. If he doesn't get help, he'll fall behind and lose a year. I know you'd do a good job. I do want to tell you though that there are two big problems: the first is that Mac lives in Meadows (a suburb about 50 miles from my house), and the second is that you won't get paid until the lawsuit is settled and that could take four or five years. So do you think you might be interested?"

Interested? I sure was. I asked Jack a lot of questions. What grade was Mac in? What kind of a student was he? Which hours and how many would I work each day? Could I at least get paid for day-to-day expenses like gas for the car and tolls? Did he have any ideas about how the principal and teachers felt about a strange person coming in to tutor one of their students, especially one from so far away?

I got some answers. I could make my own hours, work as many as I felt necessary to do a good job, and I'd get paid every two weeks for all of my out-of-pocket expenses. As for information about Mac as a student or about teachers' feelings, Jack suggested I talk to Mac's parents and the teachers themselves.

"If you think you'd be interested in this job, I'll give you the phone numbers, and I'll let everyone know you'll be calling. And, Eileen, I'd like your decision by the end of the week."

I was intrigued. Teaching a whole curriculum to one student and watching his learning processes day by day would be a new learning experience for me.

By Wednesday I had spoken with Mrs. MacArthur and Mr. Patrick, the principal of Mac's school. Mr. Patrick asked me if I knew that during the past year, most of Mac's time had been spent in Learning Disabilities and Special Education classes. Without waiting for my answer, he announced that all *he* was interested in was that Mac work on his reading and math. He didn't tell me why he felt that was so important. He ended by asking me if I could come to school to talk with all of Mac's LD and Special Ed teachers so that they could personally give me their own individual lesson plans and curriculums. We decided that on the first day that I was scheduled to see Mac, I would first stop at school to see his teachers.

I must admit I was surprised when I first heard about Special Ed and Learning Disabilities classes, but I still decided that I would like to teach Mac. I called Jack. "I'll take the job. When do I start?"

And so began my experiences with homebound students, their families and their teachers.

I remember, even as a very young child, wanting to believe that all teachers cared about each of their students individually — not just collectively — and time after time, being bitterly disappointed. If I ever had any doubts about the credibility of my feelings, they were quickly dispelled by the time I left Mac's school.

That morning I saw Mac's counselor who gave me two handbooks, Mac's schedule which did not appear to be for special classes, two math books, two social studies books, a reading test for Mac, and work sheets for almost every subject. I was inundated with books and papers! I never saw so much stuff for one eighth grade student in my entire teaching career! And that work was for a student in regular classes. There was *nothing, absolutely nothing* for a student in Special Ed or Learning Disabilities classes. I left the counselor's office and went to see Mac's teachers. First I saw the science teacher who showed me what book the class was using. She alone had a special book for learning disabled students. The book was written on a 3.5 grade reading level but had the same content as the regular eighth grade science book. She gave me a copy and asked me to check in with her every couple of weeks. I wondered if that was to make sure she kept control. I went to the math teacher who said, "Just follow my lesson plans on this sheet." This math teacher was a very young and very new teacher.

The social studies teacher was terrific. He said that, although he had always used the traditional method of teaching, this year he was going to use contracts and independent learning. "This is new for me," he said, "so that I really don't have any long range lesson plans to give you." He did give me some for the first few weeks and told me to work at a pace that was good for Mac, then check in with him if I wanted to. The reading teacher gave me a stack of remedial cards and sighed, "He doesn't read well at all."

Every teacher said I should grade Mac every 6 weeks and bring the grades to school to be recorded. And they all wished me luck!

As I was walking towards the entrance of the school, classes let out and I nearly got trampled by a herd of students dashing to their next classes. One of them took heart and helped me out to the car with my load of books.

For a few minutes, I sat quietly in my car reviewing what had just happened. Curriculums? Was there one for Special Ed? I didn't have one. Lesson plans? There weren't any for a student who needed special help. I knew I would have to make my own.

I did learn one bit of information: the principal didn't want Mac to come back to school because he thought Mac might trip or fall during changes in classes. Boy, I sure knew what he meant!

I sat there surrounded by books and papers and laden with feelings: feelings of abandonment for me as well as for Mac; feelings of anger because it seemed like no one cared about Mac as a person; and with feelings of curiosity — just what was Mac really like?

I drove into an older, somewhat shabby but neat part of town. Houses needed painting, lawns were patchy and uneven and some of the curbs were broken. I found that out when I drove right into one. As I knocked on the screened door, hoping all the books and papers wouldn't come tumbling down, an unsmiling, blonde boy on crutches limped from inside the house. "Mac? I'm Mrs. Shapiro."

Wordlessly he opened the door, led me inside, and sat down at the dining room table. He just sat there, looking forlorn and alone. He was alone; his mother and sisters were at work or at school, and his father, who was on disability, had left the house.

I tried to start a conversation, but Mac wouldn't talk. "Maybe," I thought, "Mac is quiet because I'm a stranger. Or maybe he just doesn't like to talk!" So I told him that I had visited his school, talked to his teachers, and picked up his books. I also mentioned that the teachers had not told me what Mac was supposed to have learned in each subject. "So," I asked, "would you mind doing some math problems to show me how much you really do know and where you may need help?"

He answered me with a slight nod of his head. I took that as an okay. Then I asked him to read a short passage on one of the cards his English teacher had given me and then answer the questions that followed the paragraph. This time I heard an almost imperceptible grunt that sounded like consent. I felt a little better. At least, I thought, Mac was hearing me!

I gave him a range of problems in addition, subtraction, multiplication and division. While he did those, I began to write some others in fractions, decimals, percents. I glanced up and noticed Mac biting his lip. He had finished most of the problems quickly but was having difficulty doing long division. I stopped him, saying, "Why don't we see how you're doing? You sure finished those first problems quickly!"

He gave me his paper and I found that he could add and subtract with no problems. And he could multiply most numbers together. He was stymied when he had to multiply by sevens or eights. And although he could do most multiplication easily, he could do very little long division. "It's hard," he groaned. He was quiet for a minute and then his face brightened up. "Division is hard, but I can do decimals. Ea—sy!"

"Great! I'll write a few and you can show me how good you are!" I expected him to have trouble with the decimal points, but he surprised me. He knew!

After a few more minutes, I discovered that Mac could do simple fractions with common denominators but not problems with different denominators. I stopped there. I could see what my lesson plans for math would be.

About an hour after we began working together, Mac started to open up. "I hate being home," he said. "I miss my friends. The doctors won't let me out of the house except to their offices, and my friends won't come over here. There's nothing to do and besides..." he hesitated and then continued, "they know my dad doesn't like them." There was a pregnant pause. "I hate school," he said. "And they don't care if I come to school or not."

I asked who "they" was. "The teachers. They don't call to see how I am. They never even called when I was in the hospital. And you know what? I used to ditch school, and they never even called home."

I had heard kids say things like this before, so I decided to probe a little deeper. "So after you ditched classes, did you do the homework you missed? Did you ask the teachers what they had done in class on those days?"

"Never! I hate school and I hate all that work! They go too fast for me, and they don't care if I learn it or not!"

Oh, boy. I had a feeling this was not going to be easy.

I gave Mac a reading card. He read the passage to himself. It was written at about fourth grade level, yet it took him a long time to finish it. When he was done, he looked up. "Okay, I read it. Now what?"

"Can you answer the questions on the card?"

He squinted at the paper. "Uh-h-h. I can't remember the answer to this question. I don't even know what they want me to say."

Now I really knew this was going to be a tough job. I had to find out if Mac didn't understand the questions or if he really didn't know what he had read. I soon found out that Mac could read the words and could understand the simply stated facts, but he could not read between the lines.

Little by little I was beginning to understand Mac's frustrations about school. I could sense his loneliness.

I decided to make it a short day, so after two hours, I told Mac I would return the next day and we'd look at the science and social studies books. Mac almost smiled at me when I said goodbye.

It was a long trip to Mac's home and back. It took an hour each way. The first half of the trip to his house was on a very busy toll road; the second half was on an almost deserted one. I remember thinking that if I ever got a flat tire or ran out of gas on that second part of the trip, I'd really be stuck. Few cars used that route and I could be stranded for a very long time.

As I drove home, thinking about the unthinkable, I decided the best way to put potential problems out of my mind would be to talk into a cassette recorder...to tape everything that had happened during the time I had spent with Mac whether it was about Mac himself, the things we were doing, or the interactions between him, me and his parents. Little did I realize that I would also be taping myself muttering, sometimes very angrily, to other drivers, laughing with the people at the tollbooths, and talking to myself! I also didn't realize that when Mac went back to school, I would have 18 hours of tape with some terrific and innovative ideas for teaching that would someday be enough material for a book but much too much for a chapter. Therefore, I'm only going to touch on some of my experiences with Mac.

Mac's dad was in and out of the house every day. I was uncomfortable with him around because I felt a vague uneasiness every time he talked to me. After each of our lessons, he would make comments like, "How is Mac doing? Is he doing his homework? He'd better because no son of mine is going to shirk his duties. He must do everything you tell him to or he'll answer to me!" Mr MacArthur then told me about Joe, his older son, and *his* problems in school. The boy had been expelled and Mr. MacArthur was trying to get him re-enrolled. Mr. MacArthur was very upset with the school system; he didn't feel it was fair for Joe to have been expelled even though he had ignored many of the rules of the school.

Mr. MacArthur was also upset with Mac's friends whom he felt were not only derelict with their homework but also were a bad influence on Mac. They stayed up late, overslept in the mornings and were late to school a good deal of the time.

My own belief was that Mr. MacArthur himself was not a great role model. He told me about the minor injuries he incurred at almost every job he held; he said he had received workers' compensation on and off for quite a while. He hadn't held a permanent job in many, many months nor did it appear that he was even looking for one.

I met Mac's mother only once. She worked at a nearby motel and I went there to learn what I could about Mac's injury. Was it ever so painful that Mac wouldn't be able to do his homework? Her answer was no. I already knew the answer to the next question, but I wanted to hear it from her. Did Mac want to go back to school? And of course I heard what I expected to hear. "No." She sounded sad when she answered. I spoke to Mrs. MacArthur only a few times in the next months; most of my contacts were with Mac's father.

On my second day with Mac, he read from the science book about the human body. We did the first lesson together so that I could watch him. He was interested in the content and because it was easy to read, he did that lesson well. He even seemed to like doing it! I assigned the next lesson for homework.

Then Mac opened the social studies book...and his jaw dropped! The type was small and the reading difficult. The book covered American history and began with Columbus and his discovery of America. Mac, I saw, knew very little geography and had very little concept of cause and effect. He did not know the meaning of several words and so lost much of his concentration as he struggled with the text.

I stopped him. "You know," I said, "I have an idea that maybe the company that publishes your science book also publishes one about American history which will be easier to read. I'll call them later, so let's put history on hold for a while."

Mac's face lost its tension and he relaxed. "Okay!"

We spent the next few minutes just talking. He asked about my family and learned that I had four children, the youngest of whom was also in the 8th grade. Mac seemed upset. "I bet he's smart and can read and can do math and ..."

I interrupted him. "Everyone's different, Mac. You can learn too. If you put your mind to it, you can do anything you want to do."

Mac needed all the encouragement and assurance I could give him, and for six months, I gave as much as I could.

That afternoon I called the publishers of Mac's science book and found that they did indeed print American history and geography books at Mac's reading level, and so I ordered them. I wrote the lesson plans and some worksheets for the next day. Some of my worksheets included maps of Southern Europe and the Mediterranean Sea on which Mac was to write the names of the countries, cities and rivers. Others contained lists of words to break up into syllables, to sound out and to learn to spell. Spelling was an important subject. If Mac couldn't spell, how could he write well? And if he couldn't write well, how could he make anyone understand what he was trying to say?

Every day we also worked on Mac's reading comprehension. We started at a 3.5 reading level; it took several weeks before he advanced to the 4.0 level. I brought comic strips, comic books, and newspaper articles that were simply written. I wrote very short stories and asked him to write endings. My goal was to make sure that Mac could read, write and spell well enough to ensure his getting a decent job when he graduated from high school.

We worked on history and social studies, and I spent a lot of time on geography because I wanted Mac to be aware of the world he was living in. We discussed the news and what was happening in different parts of the world.

Working with Mac was sometimes very frustrating, but always interesting. To see one student grow, day by day, was fascinating. Teaching Mac sharpened my skills; it was as if I were on trial every day as a teacher. What I learned from Mac I was able to use with my other students. I became more determined than ever not to let any of my students get lost in the shuffle, to fall behind, or lose confidence in themselves.

What do I say to those of you interested in teaching students who cannot go to school? Talk to the your students' teachers, then go to the students' homes, watch and listen. It doesn't take long to get a feel for their home life and the family relationships. Watch for comings and goings and possible interruptions. Study your students closely to see what they like and dislike, how they learn, how they study, and most important, how they feel about being out of school because of their injuries or illnesses. The more information you collect, the easier your job will be.

But about Mac. At the end of our six months together, Mac had progressed to percents and word problems in math. He was reading better and understanding more; social studies and history made more sense. He had mixed feelings about going back to school: he didn't like the idea of going back to classes, but he was eager to be back with kids his own age.

When the lawyers told me that Mac was well enough to go back to school, I was a bit relieved. The driving and the long hours had finally gotten to me. I almost felt like I was getting a vacation!

Mac and I had a touching farewell. We had become friends and had talked about many things. He had remarked that he was unhappy at home and felt alone and ignored much of the time. He liked his mother and sisters but didn't get along with his dad. He mentioned moving west when he graduated from high school.

I told Mac that I hoped he would have someone to talk to after I left, someone who would listen and understand. I also told him that I hoped things would be better for him in school, but if he ever needed help, he should feel free to call me. We said we'd keep in touch, but we didn't.

Mac's lawsuit came to trial almost six years to the day after we parted, and two hours before the trial began, his case was settled out of court. Mac was 20 years old. He said that he was finally getting away from his father; he and his girl were leaving for Colorado shortly. He sounded relieved that he was able to get on with his life. I wished him well. I hope some of his dreams are coming true.

## Chapter Eight

# Nick, a High School Dropout

Nick first came to see me in August, just before the beginning of the school year. He was eighteen years old and had dropped out of school two years earlier, at the end of his sophomore year. He arrived with his mother, a smiling but determined woman.

"As I told you on the phone," she began, "Nick had trouble in school. He felt ignored when he asked for help; it seems many of his teachers didn't want to take time to figure out what was wrong and work with him." Mrs. Randall was disturbed. "They just sent him away to another school for help in English and then left him to his own devices in all the rest of his classes. Nick got so frustrated and disillusioned that he just left school. Now he wants to learn and his father and I want to give him that opportunity. Can you help him?"

Nick was tall and good-looking. He was also shy and introverted. He sat looking at the floor while his mother talked, but now his face was tense, waiting for my answer.

"I'm sure I can help," I replied. "We can meet twice a week, Nick, if that's okay with you and your folks." They both nodded. "Good. Each day after studying together, I'm going to give you homework. I realize it's going to be hard to get back into the scheme of things because you've been out of school for a while. Do you think you can work out a schedule of some sort to do the work?"

He murmured something unintelligible, and I had to strain to hear his words. "Um-hm. I'll try."

# Nick, a High School Dropout

His mother seemed pleased. "Fine," she said quietly. She stood up, told Nick she'd be back in 50 minutes and left my office.

I hoped that since we were now alone, Nick might talk a little more openly, so I asked *him* to tell me how he felt about his schooling.

"I hated it." He spoke very quietly. "I can't remember the last time everything was okay. I know I must have some kind of reading problem, but no one ever seemed to care. The teachers just passed me from one grade to the next without doing much to help me. And when I got to high school, things got even worse! Everyone must have decided I didn't read well enough even for their basic classes so they sent me to a nearby teachers' college for reading and grammar. But you know what was dumb? That class met during regular school hours, so I was always missing math or social studies. I hated that!"

Nick took a deep breath and sighed. He looked exhausted from saying so much. I could feel his frustration. I thought for a moment and then said, "Well, how about you and I starting with reading and grammar?" He nodded imperceptibly.

"Great! I'd like you to write a very short paragraph about any sport you like. Will you do that?"

Nick looked up almost terror stricken. "Very, very short," I repeated. "Maybe eight or nine lines."

So Nick started to write, stopping every few minutes to think. Then he handed his paper to me guardedly. As I read it, I noticed that he wrote "how" for "who," his grammar was poor, but the anecdote itself was clever. And so I told him what a good writer he was, adding that his grammar and spelling needed work. I then asked him if he would mind reading aloud a paragraph in one of the literature books I had. He grimaced but agreed. As he read, I saw the kinds of reading problems he had were similar to those when he wrote. He reversed words. For example, he said "was" when he meant "saw." But when I asked questions

**87**

about the story itself, he answered everything correctly; there was no lack of comprehension.

I wondered if Nick had a form of dyslexia and decided to work on that premise. I had seen books written for teaching people with this disability and I decided to order them. Meanwhile, I asked Nick to read the first three chapters of a book that was usually assigned to juniors in high school; this particular edition was written at a lower grade level. I also gave him some spelling words to learn. We then scheduled our sessions for the next few weeks. Nick didn't smile when he left. He just muttered his goodby.

As soon as he left, I contacted a group that did research on dyslexia and published books on the subject. It is called Orton-Gillingham and its homebase is in Boston. When I asked for a catalog of all the books that were published, the customer service representative said that there were staff people in these offices who would try to answer any of my questions and give me advice immediately. I explained what I thought was Nick's problem, and they advised me which books to order. "If they are not helpful," they said, "return them for credit and we'll help you find the right ones."

With that kind of attitude, I thought, I couldn't go wrong, so I ordered several books and workbooks for Nick.

Nick said very little the first few weeks we worked together. Much of the time he sat hunched over the table as he read or wrote. He nodded his head when I asked questions that required a simple yes, and he shook it quickly when he felt I had said something wrong. But he was eager to learn and he did most of his homework.

It isn't easy teaching someone who doesn't say much, like Nick. Sometimes I feel like I am alone in the room. I enjoy teaching more when there is a repartee between my students and me. It makes for a freer, more congenial hour. The very rare times when my husband has to interrupt our sessions to ask me an important question, he gives a warm hello to my students with an apology for disturbing us, and often they don't even look up. For months, Nick acted this way.

Then suddenly it was the middle of October and the governor's political race was heating up in our state. Being eighteen, Nick could vote. I decided to stray from our work, and I asked him how he felt about the elections. It was like a flood dam burst! Nick was an avid Republican. He loved our governor, and thought he was doing a fabulous job. He started to give me all the arguments for retaining this man: his great past accomplishments as well as his wonderful future plans. Nick was really into politics. We spent an extra half hour just debating the pros and cons of the candidates. Nick's face was flushed with an excitement that he had kept well hidden until then.

That conversation broke the ice. Nick started to talk about himself a little more. He was upset about not having a high school degree. He didn't like feeling different from his friends who had graduated and were away at college. He wanted to read all the books on the high school juniors' and seniors' curriculum, so we made up a list of those books and Nick began his program. We had concentrated on English for about three months when Nick said to me, "I've been thinking. I'd like to review math again. I had difficulty with that, too. Could we work on that?"

I gave him some math problems to do and found that he had fallen behind in school when he had to learn percents and ratios. He didn't know much about algebra and had never learned any geometry.

We added arithmetic to our schedule and found that two sessions a week weren't covering all that we were doing. Nick was already reading books, writing stories, working on spelling and grammar, and now we were adding math. I asked him if he thought his parents might let him come for a third session each week.

He believed they would. I called his parents and got an okay to set up another hour.

Slowly I was learning about Nick. He loved to sketch; sometimes he would draw cars or designs of houses. Often he brought homework sheets completely covered with doodles. One day he told me he had built a model of a house.

"Do you think," he asked timorously, "that I could learn to be an architect someday? I think that's what I'd like to do."

"Why not?" And I encouraged him to hang on to his dream.

Nick's reading and writing was improving. His comprehension of whatever book he was reading was great; he had started reading "Hamlet" and Nick and his father enjoyed discussing it together. Although Nick still confused words when he read, I decided not to make too big an issue of the problem; it didn't seem to hinder him too much.

Several months after I had started seeing Nick, I opened the envelope in which his dad always put his check, and a note dropped out. It said simply, "We're very proud of Nick's accomplishments. Thank you."

Nick learned the basic math concepts and we moved on to basic algebra. Nick understood the material while he was in my office and did all the examples correctly, but if he did the homework the next day, he would forget what he had learned. He knew arithmetic well, so I turned variables into real numbers and simplified the algebra problems. I did it like this: "Jane cuts each of (n + 3) pies into 5 pieces. In terms of n, what is the total number of pieces of pie?"

The problem written like this confused Nick. When I asked Nick to put in a real number like 6 instead of (n + 3) and cut 6 pies into 5 pieces each, how many pieces of pie would he get? He immediately answered 30. "How did you get 30?" I asked.

"By multiplying 6 times 5."

"Okay. So if you multiply 6 times 5, why can't you multiply (n + 3) times 5?" Nick looked confused again. "Multiplication is reciprocal, remember?  6 x 5 = 5 x 6.

# Nick, a High School Dropout

When you write 5 times (n + 3), it looks like this: 5(n + 3). Now multiply 5 times n, then 5 times 3 and add them together to get 5n +15."

Nick smiled. "They sure like to trick you, don't they? They like to make it look so hard and you make it so easy." And gradually Nick understood all the concepts and remembered them from lesson to lesson.

Nick and I were becoming friends. He smiled more often, sat straighter in his chair and sometimes he even said hello to my husband. After our sessions were over, we would sit and talk. We discussed everything: the news, national and international, movies and television, cars, sports. He talked about his family; he had an older brother at home and several sisters either married or away at school. He was close to his parents. He and his dad loved to discuss books and world news. His dad was very interested in everything Nick and I were doing together.

Nick looked forward to college breaks. He and his friends always got together and had fun times. They all loved to camp out and this summer they were driving west and camping there. It was always hard when his friends went back to their respective colleges.

I decided to bring up the idea of Nick's taking the high school equivalency test. Until now he had only had one goal in mind: completing some of the courses he would have taken in high school.

"With a General Education Degree (GED)," I informed him, "you can apply to many colleges and universities. It does mean, however, that to get your GED, you have to pass a test in math, including algebra and geometry, reading, English grammar, spelling, social studies and science. It's a lot of work, but I know you can do it if you want to. What do you think? And of course we'd have to talk to your parents because I think you'd have to come more than three times a week."

College? I could see Nick's face light up with anticipation. "I'll ask them as soon as Dad gets home. Could I let you know the next time I come?"

When he came for his next session, Nick was elated. His parents had given the go-ahead and they were excited for him. We decided to meet every day and move steadily toward his goal.

I have several different sets of GED workbooks. These books are readily available from most textbook publishers; some are easier than others and some are more comprehensive. You have to know your students and fit the books to each one's ability.

I reviewed all the books and chose one that was clear and concise. It also was a book with questions covering all the subjects of the GED with explanations for the all the answers, right or wrong. To be sure that I had chosen correctly, I had Nick work some of the English grammar and reading questions. He understood them and was able to do the work without too much difficulty. And so we began.

There is a pre-test in most books that allows both tutor and student to see in which areas the student needs help. Because Nick and his dad talked about politics and world news a lot of the time, Nick knew much about geography. I mentioned many countries, and he could place most of them on a map. Pinpointing countries in Indonesia was difficult because there are so many, large and small, huddled together. African countries were also hard to learn because many on the continent were in a seemingly constant state of flux, changing their names and government leaders very often. But Nick loved the challenge. We discussed climates and economies; together we learned more about the different cultures. We even touched on the politics of many countries and how they related to each other. We spent several weeks working on Social Studies and I must admit I, too, learned a great deal from these sessions.

# Nick, a High School Dropout

Science was hard because we didn't have a lab to work with. But I had a kitchen. One day we mixed vinegar and baking powder together to create a kind of white lava pouring over the cup. We wrote out the equations to show why the elements acted and reacted as they did. Another time I bought two beakers, telling Nick to fill only one with a combination of salt and water. I had also bought a ball-shaped vial with two openings, one on each end, and two pieces of tubing. I then told Nick to connect the filled beaker to the ball-shaped vial with one piece of tubing and then do the same on the other side with the empty beaker. I then instructed him to put the vial with the salt water onto the stove with a medium-sized flame beneath it. As he watched, the water in the beaker began to boil and then turn to steam. The steam rose in the tubing and collected in the center vial. We went on with other work while the solution cooled. After about one half hour, we looked at the center vial and noticed that the steam was beginning to cool and was beginning to return to droplets of moisture. The moisture moved toward the second beaker which slowly filled with water. When the second beaker was full and the first empty, I asked Nick to pour the water in a cup and taste it.

"This doesn't have salt in it!" he exclaimed. "How did that happen?"

I laughed and told him the process was called desalinization of water and in some western U.S. coastal areas, there were already facilities using this technique to create good, fresh drinkable water from the ocean. "It is a very costly process," I commented. "I'll bet they're working very hard to make this a more cost-effective method, to help us have fresh water more cheaply."

Whichever experiments we could do in my kitchen, we did. It made science more palatable and in many ways, easier to understand. It was fun for me because I had to find experiments that we could do in a kitchen and researching for them was fascinating. I also told Nick to watch and see what happened when certain liquids were mixed together and what happened when certain frozen foods were defrosted in a microwave oven for too short a time—the frozen foods stayed frozen only on the outside because microwaved foods defrost from the inside out. Nick enjoyed the experiments.

His spelling still needed a lot of work so I used spelling books for dyslexics. These books helped a lot although there were many words Nick still had trouble with.

Algebra was becoming easier for Nick, and so I decided to add geometry to our schedule. Nick understood some very simple basics because of the simple plans he drew for the houses he designed. He knew about angles and parallel lines. What he needed was all the rest of the geometry theorems! Again, because I had several geometry books, I could choose the best book for Nick. Geometry can be very hard for many students. I have found many students who do well in algebra and dislike geometry intensely, and others who do just the opposite. Nick loved geometry. It was easy for him to visualize all the different polygons and angles. What was hard for him to remember from day to day was theorems. Because he was with me for private tutoring, I could go more slowly, show him two or three different ways to do a problem, and then Nick could choose which one was the easiest for him. Luckily we didn't have to work out proofs. They weren't necessary for the GED. What we did need to work on was how the rules were written and why they worked as they did — which was no easy assignment. But we had five days a week, up to one and a half hours a day to study together.

Nick was fun to work with. I love individual tutoring. I can watch each person work and correct his mistakes, explaining why as we go along. I can show him where to start a problem and then let him finish with me watching over his shoulder. Watching a student learn and build self-confidence always makes me glow!

# Nick, a High School Dropout

Nick was now less shy and more confident; he sat straighter, smiled more, and said a warm "hello" to my husband when he saw him.

After 10 months I sensed it was getting close to GED time, so I started giving Nick a quiz in one of the subjects of the GED each time we met. I wanted to observe his reactions to the questions. After a few weeks it was clear that it was time for the test itself. Nick felt ready to take the it; he had worked hard and long and was sure of himself.

We began our goodbyes. After two years, it wasn't easy. We had worked so closely for so long! Although I know my students must be on their way and on their own, it feels like I'm losing a friend when a student like Nick leaves. Many of my students have the same problem: they feel the break too. We're proud of what we've done together, we know we've reached our goals, but even so, after a long period of togetherness, it takes a few sessions to wish each other well and say our final farewells.

A short time later, I was on vacation in California. I called into my answering machine and heard Nick say he had passed the GED test. I could "hear" the smile on his voice. I immediately called him to congratulate him. He was so excited!

And then I had a nice surprise! Nick called to ask me if he could come back for a few sessions to review one of the college entrance exams — the ACT. As if he had to ask!

We worked for about two months until Nick took the test. Although I have not heard from Nick since then, I have always felt that he must have received a good enough score to get into a college.

I bumped into a friend of his a few years later who told me that Nick had a very good position in an architectural firm in a nearby suburb and was very happy. And isn't that what tutoring is all about?

## Chapter Nine

# Teaching Study Skills

L earning study skills is probably the most important lesson for all students. They can listen, take notes, and ask questions, but if they don't have the study skills, they are in trouble. Their work is often not clear, ideas are not understood, and when they have to take tests, they become extremely anxious.

Teaching study skills is somewhat different at the elementary school level from middle and high school. With any child you have to start with an anecdote or story, anything to excite their interest. Years ago, I wrote two study skills books for the Chicago Tribune which were given out to a half million students in the Chicago metropolitan area. The outlines for the booklets were almost identical, but a number of changes were made because of the ages of the students.

This chapter incorporates a good deal of the content of those booklets.

## Listening

Because listening is so important for younger children, I ask them these questions:

"Would you believe that listening is a skill? It takes a lot of work to listen well. Too many people just daydream when they think they are listening. They miss a lot of information.

"Has something like this ever happened to you? It's Monday and dinner time, and your family is altogether. 'I have some terrific news,' you begin. There's a carnival at school Saturday, and I have a part in a play. Everyone's invited, and I want you to come!

"Your family smiles, excited for you, and says, 'How great!'

"On Thursday, you remind everybody about the carnival. 'What carnival? What play?' says one member of your family. 'When did you say it was?' says another. 'I just made an appointment to have my hair cut!"

Then I ask my students to think about why this happened. Because no one was really listening. We then compare that story with what happens in school. Do they remember a time when their lesson wasn't ready because they didn't hear which day it was due? Do they remember getting a low grade on a test because they didn't listen during class discussions?

The kids then make a list of what they believe they should do in class. They come up with all kinds of ideas, but in the end they realize which are the important rules to follow:

1.  keeping their eyes on their classroom teacher;
2.  sitting up straight, and keeping their desks neat with only the items they need at any time;
3.  not talking to classmates while the teacher is speaking;
4.  taking part in discussions because this forces them to listen;
5.  writing assignments in a notebook.

## Following Directions

Following directions is probably the second most important rule for students. For the younger students, you can use the game of "Simon Says" to illustrate what happens when they don't follow directions...in the game or in school. And they need to learn to look at directions written on the pages of their books. Sometimes in math books a page is printed with many problems on it. On the top of the page the word add is printed, and halfway down the directions change and the word subtract is printed. Often children begin adding and get so caught up in it that they fail to see the change in directions. When they correct their papers and see how many problems they've gotten wrong, they are confused and don't understand why their scores are so low until someone points out their mistake in not looking for directions.

## Neatness

Students often keep every piece of paper they've written, every page of homework, every essay, every assignment sheet, every scrap of paper in their notebooks. It doesn't matter how old they are, how torn they are, nor how crumpled. The papers are just tossed in the notebook helter skelter. And then when the students have to find an important homework paper or an assignment sheet, they have difficulty extracting it.

It is extremely important that these students learn to keep a neat notebook by sorting out the old papers. If they are determined to keep the old papers, tell them to put them in a box or folder and leave them at home. And even then they should clean out those files every 3 to 4 weeks. They have to understand the advantages of a clean notebook, such as the amount of time they'll save looking for assignments and homework, and then they'll change those old habits more easily.

Can you imagine the myriad of messy papers teachers have to cope with? Kids will use a heavy black leaded pencil and when they erase, the papers stay dirty and messy from the lead. The writing does not erase neatly or cleanly. Kids write over numbers and letters, thinking the darker they write over, the easier it will be to see. Some just scribble and don't care.

The students I see learn that the papers they hand in with their names on them are an indication of who they are. If the papers are sloppy, teachers often feel that the kids don't care about their work, that maybe they're sloppy in *everything* they do. Once their names are on the papers, students must learn that they are telling a lot about themselves. I'll even demonstrate for students what their teachers, friends, and relatives see by my scribbling or writing over or erasing poorly just like they do and then asking them to try to read what I've written.

Students fundamentally want to be neat but too many teachers don't say anything to them or write notes on their papers or tell their parents. Therefore, it is up to you as their tutor to help them. Kids appreciate your help to learn to be neater and more organized. This help makes them feel better about themselves.

## A Place to Study

When kids first come and you ask them where they do their homework, you'll get answers from "on the kitchen table," "in the family room on the floor" to "in my bedroom" and "at the library."

Many times I will ask my students to picture this scene:

> You've just sat down to study, opened your books, and begun to read, when suddenly the doorbell rings. Your sister or brother shouts, 'I'll get it!' and runs to the door. The dog starts barking, your mother calls out, 'Who is it, Johnny?', and the reply is a shout, a door is slammed, and then there is either relative quiet...or even more commotion!

And you're trying to study? Impossible unless you're wearing ear plugs or very heavy earmuffs! And that can become very uncomfortable after a while, besides really not being a good way to learn. For these reasons, it is very important that you find a place to study that is quiet and with no distractions.

I tell my students that there are two main choices for a place to study: their homes or the library. If they like to work at home, they have to realize that other people live there too. And so phones and doorbells ring, and people come and go.

Since you are their tutor, you can help them figure out a place where they can concentrate without interruptions, and the best place is usually in their bedrooms, where they will need a desk or table, good lighting, *and* a lot of willpower to keep from lying down on their beds to study. There are always some students who believe they can lie down on their beds and really concentrate. Then before they know it, they begin to doze off or daydream, and their best intentions have fled. So some rules for studying in a bedroom are:

1. don't study on your bed
2. don't make phone calls unless you are stuck and feel a classmate can help.
3. don't watch television while you study.

There are kids who don't like to be working shut away from people. Ask them to have their parents help them find a good place. Because parents want their students to excel, they'll usually cooperate eagerly. But be sure to remind the students that even if they find a quiet spot, it's in the open and they're going to have to concentrate harder. Tell them to watch their grades, and if they aren't as good as they should be, it may be that people are walking around or the phone is ringing, or a number of other reasons.

If they find that there are just too many distractions at home, suggest the library. Studying at the library has many advantages and one disadvantage. The disadvantage is that students have to travel to and from the library, but the advantages are great. It is usually very quiet. Carrels are set up away from traffic and busy areas, and the atmosphere there breeds studying and learning.

The library also has almost all the reference books students might need for their work. There are dictionaries, encyclopedias of all kinds, atlases, thesauruses, and new and old periodicals. Libraries also have reference librarians who are acquainted with everything in the building. Students need to know that if they cannot locate the information they need, the reference librarian can guide them to it.

## Study Schedules

When it comes to study schedules, the first thing you must do is teach kids to write down all their assignments in a dated assignment book or spiral notebook. I have had students who wrote their assignments down on sheets of paper and then lost or misplaced those sheets. Suddenly these students remember that an assignment is due the next day and they don't have the information they need, or they remember that there is a test the next day and then panic because they haven't studied for it.

Once you have helped them break that bad habit, you can help them make a good, workable study schedule. That means not only studying in the same place every day, but studying at the same regular time each day. Have them make a chart like the one on the following page.

|  | Monday | Tuesday | Wednesday | Thursday | Friday |
|---|---|---|---|---|---|
| 4:00 |  |  |  |  |  |
| 4:30 |  |  |  |  |  |
| 5:00 |  |  |  |  |  |
| 5:30 |  |  |  |  |  |
| 6:00 |  |  |  |  |  |
| 6:30 |  |  |  |  |  |
| 7:00 |  |  |  |  |  |
| 7:30 |  |  |  |  |  |
| 8:00 |  |  |  |  |  |
| 8:30 |  |  |  |  |  |
| 9:00 |  |  |  |  |  |

These are the usual hours after school. Have them fill in, if possible, the dinner hour and their weekly commitments, such as dance lessons, football practice, work hours, and any other times that are filled. Then show them where they have free time to study. It may be the same on Monday and Thursday and different on the other days, but those hours should be committed to studying. It's important to tell them to take a break every hour for 10 minutes or so and then go right back to work. If they take "just a minute" to check the news on TV or radio, they may put off returning to work and then fall behind in their studies.

On the other hand, make sure they make a reasonable plan. They may fill in three to four hours of study a day with no breaks, phone calls and no time outs. That schedule is sometimes overwhelming, so they most likely won't stick to it. After all, not only are they students, but also social individuals. All work and no play *does* make Jack a dull boy.

You can also remind them that there are always a few extra minutes they can use for studying like the times waiting for appointments, rides and buses.

## Reading Textbook Skills

I have mentioned many skills in previous chapters, but there are many I haven't. There is a good way to teach the kids how to read a textbook and how to retain that knowledge. Authors of textbooks plan their layouts carefully. Most material, as you know, is written in an orderly manner — from first to last, from beginning to end. And the authors' use of graphs and pictures is used to make the material more clear. They use bold-faced headings to point out the ideas that will be most important; they often write questions at the end of sections in a chapter and most of the time there are questions at the end of the chapter for review.

Have your students first find out what a chapter is about. Tell them to look at the title, look at pictures and graphs and read the comments beneath them, and then read the questions at the end of the chapter. That gives them an idea of what they should look for as they read. Now they can read the chapter. As they read, tell them to answer any questions as they go along. Tell them to answer the questions at the end of the chapter and lastly, if at all possible, tell them to study with a friend or two—ones who are intelligent and care as much as they do. It's a known fact that people remember more when they not only read the material but hear it spoken aloud.

Teach the kids how to underline and how to take notes. Most kids underline too much and then don't know what to study. If they own the textbooks, remind them that they can write notes in the margins of the books, but if they don't own their books, they should take notes on index cards. A good idea is to write the book titles and page numbers on the cards so they can easily find the pages if necessary.

Impress upon your students how great flash cards are. I always advise the kids who are studying for the SAT to write the words they don't know on cards. All of them say, "Sure" and even promise they will. And the next week most of them haven't written even one card. Then the week before the test they are anxious and intimidated by all the words they don't know. Once during the first sessions of two different classes I handed out a package of index cards to each of my students and only two or three out of 16 used them; those few who did were excited because they had learned so many new words.

## Reference Books

I once had a student who had to write a paper on World War I. I gave him a "W" book from a set of 1939 encyclopedias. He searched and searched and complained, "I can't find anything in this book about that war. Don't the writers of this encyclopedia think it was important? All I can find is a section about a World War."

I was amused and tried not to show it. I asked him in what year the books were written. He checked and answered, "1939." And when asked when World War II began, he answered 1941. "So," I asked, "how many world wars had there been before 1941?"

He thought about that for a few minutes and then replied, "Only one."

"Well, if that is so, doesn't it stand to reason that there was no need for a number in 1939?"

He grinned sheepishly, opened the book once again, and found all the information he needed.

Sometimes because some reference books like encyclopedias are written before a lot of new history is made, they will contain more about an earlier event. In these cases older encyclopedias and reference books, if they are available, are sometimes more useful than up-to-date ones.

# Teaching Study Skills

Most students know about thesauruses and almanacs. This is a good list of other references that students rarely think about:

1. *The Congressional Quarterly Weekly* — information about Congress
2. Facts on File — a catalog of news events
3. *General Sciences Index* — information about sciences
4. *McGraw-Hill Science and Technology Encyclopedia* — science  data
5. *Readers' Guide to Periodical Literature* — listing of recent magazine articles in general circulation
6. *Statistical Abstract of the United States* — government gathered statistics
7. *U.S. Government Manual* — government data.
8. Libraries usually have indices to their local newspapers. Often they are published monthly by the paper and then sent to the library. For example, the *Chicago Tribune* not only publishes this index monthly but every three months publishes a quarterly index which replaces the three monthly editions. At the end of the year, the *Tribune* publishes a bound issue for the preceding 12 months. The information is listed by subject matter, and each listing has a mini-heading, which is a description of the article. In the back of the book is a listing of names. If someone is looking for facts about a particular person, he or she can look there and find the listing for all the references about that person. It's possible your library may have information like this.

Teaching study skills is an art. Too many tutors ignore this and just tutor for daily lessons. But when students learn these skills, they do their work more successfully.

## Chapter Ten

# What If I Flunk?
# Handling Test Anxieties

"I don't understand what the matter is. Jack is so bright. He gets A's and B's on all of his homework and the teacher always tells him that his oral work is terrific. Yet he consistently gets C's or lower on his tests. And he really does study. I know because I've watched him. I just don't understand."

What touching words, and yet they are so common. "A" students in high school get low SAT and ACT scores. And elementary grade students who normally do very well in regular schoolwork do poorly in competency tests. Their chapter test grades are poor. All of these students know they "freeze" on tests but can't understand why. So they or their parents come to you for help.

When these students talk to you about tests, they'll usually tell you:

➢ how hard they've studied;

➢ the tests are impossible; the teacher asks everything except what the class has studied;

➢ they figured the test was only a quiz and it didn't count too much so they glossed over it;

➢ they spent so much time on the first or second question, they never even got to the last questions;

➢ they didn't read the questions carefully;

➢ they were so tired or anxious or worried, they just couldn't concentrate;

➢ there wasn't enough time;

➢ they forgot about it and didn't study.

## What If I Flunk?  Handling Test Anxieties

But these are not the only elements in this problem. There is often an underlying problem that stems from their homes. The kids are told that they must bring home A's or B's. They have been doing well on day-to-day homework and class work. There is no pressure, no definite amount of time allotted, and no competition with other students for grades. So, in their daily work, taking their time and being relaxed, many students do fine. Then test time comes and they hear, "We expect an A." Imagine the pressure and anxiety now!

Often the students don't understand the daily work once they've left school. Mary was learning long division in class. When her teacher sat next to her, she did fine. But when she did her homework, she was confused and didn't know what to do. Her teacher kept saying, "All Mary needs is confidence. She can do the work; she does fine when I sit next to her." Unfortunately that wasn't true. So she worked on long division with me, learning the directions outlined in the math chapter. The first session she started to get a glimmer, during the second she was doing most of the work on her own, and the third week she could do it all. Mary's teacher had not taken time to see if Mary understood all the steps in long division.

It is up to you to ferret out the difficulties that these students are having, and then help them solve the problems so that they can become successful at taking tests.

The following are some of the solutions that I have found over the years. When they say, "I studied so hard; I just don't understand why I did so poorly" or "The teacher asked questions we didn't study!" I ask *how* they studied. Have they been studying every day or were they very casual with their schoolwork, waiting until the last few days to really cram? Do they genuinely understand the material? Have they really listened in class, and concentrated on the discussions? Have they asked a question if a point was confusing, or did they just let it pass? If they were told to take notes, *did* they and were the notes legible? After determining that students are failing because of their study habits, we set up a study schedule.

When this is done, we get down to the business of studying. I look at the material my students have just read; I ask if they have any notes that I can see. After looking them over, I ask questions. If answers are confused, or completely wrong, or if they give no answers at all, they realize how poorly they are studying. So, I have them read something aloud, stopping after a paragraph or so, and then I ask them to tell me what they have read. I ask questions that require literal answers, some that require that the students make references, and some that require that the student see relationships, causes and effects, time lines, etc. They learn to recognize main ideas; in other words, what is important and what is extraneous.

I ask them to take notes from something I *say* so that I can watch how they take notes and I can see what they think is important. Then, if necessary, I can correct them and show them how to determine what the essential points are.

Each time students arrive, they show me their notes and tell me what they are learning. From this I can see how well they are studying and if they are improving. And when they take tests, I can see if they are really doing better or not. If not, I know I had better try another approach; not every child responds the same way. I still teach the same ideas; I just alter my methods of teaching.

What do you do if kids don't study because they feel the test is only a pop quiz — it doesn't count much anyway — and therefore they do very poorly? Explain to them how important each and every test is, how a test can show them their weak spots, and how the tests count as points toward a grade. Point out that a teacher in a classroom learns a lot about a student from quizzes. "Does the student care? Is he or she able to learn the material?" Somehow you have to get across to your students that they create an image of themselves for their teachers, and it is always best if the image is a good one.

What if the students don't finish tests on time because they spend too much time writing answers to the first few questions, or trying to figure out answers to questions they just don't know? If it's the former, it's important to show them how to allot their time so that as soon as the test is handed out, they look at the questions to see if they are essay type questions or multiple choice or fill-in. If the test consists of essay type questions, the students can divide the allotted time by the number of questions and then give that much time to each question. (It also helps if you teach them to first think about a question, make a short outline for it, and then write the answer.)

If students cannot finish a test that is a multiple choice, fill-in, or requires working out a problem, the best way to help them is to teach them to first answer the ones they know. They should put one mark in front of those they *think* they can do, and two marks in front of those they know will be difficult. That way, after they finish the ones they know, they can do the ones with one mark (the ones they are a little doubtful about). If there is time left, they can try the difficult ones (those with two marks).

The neat thing they learn is not to waste time trying those questions that are so troublesome. It takes practice and discipline not to try hard questions right away, if at all, but if *you* give very short quizzes with all kinds of questions, the kids practice this method and usually learn it.

Students who don't read the questions carefully enough miss key words such as "never," "always," "every," "not," or "all." Older students often have trouble with essay questions because they don't do what is asked in the questions. They are confused by questions that ask them to analyze or compare and contrast.

You may find that some students have studied hard and do know their material but still "freeze" on tests. I have found that the best solution to this problem is to simulate test conditions and give the students test after test on their subjects, short tests like the ones they take in school. They get so comfortable with the material and the tests that often the anxieties lessen considerably, and they do much better when testing.

Some students have a very basic problem. They know that they don't understand the material but manage to get through their regular every-day work. They can use their books daily, but when the tests are given, they are too afraid or embarrassed to admit they can't do the work. So, when they take the tests, they do poorly. Let the students know that you care very much about them and want to help. When they realize that it's okay to let down their guard and admit their problems, they free themselves to learn and move forward!

Dealing with pressures from home not only concerns working with the students, but talking with the families. As a tutor, it's very hard to explain to parents that their child is doing the best he can (if he really is) and that if they ease up a little, their child may do better. (See Chapter 13 dealing with parents.) Sometimes students do poorly to spite their parents. If that is the case, show the students why doing well is important for them, for their self-image and for their future. These are the times to build up their self-confidence. If they learn to feel good about themselves, they will be motivated to do well when they take tests.

## Chapter Eleven

# High School Dropouts, College Students and Adults

Rolando, 19 years old, was from Mexico. He worked sporadically, plowing snow from driveways in the winter and doing yard work in the summer. What he really wanted was to work in an architect's office. He was taking a class in drawing blueprints, but he needed a high school diploma to get a job.

Barbara and Jodi, who were also 19, wanted to go to college. Barbara was working for her dad in a car dealership, and she was unhappy there. Three years before she had dropped out of school because she thought she was wasting time and was unable to enjoy learning. So, at that time, school was one terrible bore. Now, after being out in the world and finding that she would prefer a different kind of job, she, like Rolando, found she needed a diploma.

Jodi had quit school and run away. She had had trouble with her parents, with her peers, and with school. Building relationships had been very difficult for her and because she was so unhappy, she had developed an eating disorder and become very overweight. Now, after working with a counselor, she had lost the excess weight and was extremely attractive. She was ready to enroll in a college, already had one chosen, but needed her high school diploma.

Mark was 44 years old, and a very successful business-man. He owned several night clubs and made a very good living, but he had dropped out of high school two months before high school graduation! Now he wanted to dabble in real estate but couldn't without his diploma.

There are as many reasons for wanting a high school diploma as there are students who want them. When they go to apply for a diploma, students learn they must take classes in geometry, algebra and English. After studying for several weeks, they must take an exam called GED (General Educational Development) test to qualify for their diplomas. These students are scared! They haven't been in school for so long, they believe they will have lots of trouble understanding math concepts and English grammar. So often they call a tutor for additional help. And because they are usually so dedicated, they do well when it comes to exam time.

When GED students sign up for their classes, they are given study and work sheets. They often buy a GED study guide that is sold in bookstores. Many publishers have printed these books, and they are readily available. The books contain not only problems to solve or readings to interpret, but also explanations for the methods used and interpretations wanted. If you have these books at hand, you can teach the required work.

Teaching is usually done slowly. Because the students are anxious, you must repeat every step as often as needed, then question them closely to make sure they fully understand what the question is asking, what method should be used, and how they should proceed to get the desired answer.

I have found that writing a short quiz to cover what I have been working on is a big help. The students become used to taking exams, learning to differentiate between problems, methods, interpretations, etc. You can alleviate a lot of their anxieties when they see that they can take a quiz without "freezing." It isn't easy to just sit and watch them when you can see they're having trouble. But it is a good lesson because they learn to work under pressure, and you, in turn, can often see exactly where they are having difficulties. Students too often rely on the old standby, "Oh, I understand — it's so clear. I'll really get a good grade on the test," and then when exam time comes, they freeze up. They may not have learned how to deal with their anxiety feelings. And you can help them with that!

Rolando is now an apprentice to an architect, Barbara is in college, and Jodi went to college in another state.

Mark worked hard, received his diploma, and then decided that he really liked his work, so stayed with his original business.

Most of my students call me after the GED exam to report on how it went, and usually they are quite positive about the outcome. When they call to say they received their diplomas, they are so thrilled, I can feel their excitement too!

College students are dedicated, too. They have goals and know the courses they must take in order to fulfill the prerequisites for those goals. And sometimes the required courses are tough. If they know they're going to have difficulties, they may call you at the beginning of the semester. They sometimes feel that it's "not right" to need help in college, so they are a little hesitant when they call to ask questions.

"Uh, do you teach physics — for college level? I'm going to need this course and it sure isn't one of my better subjects! You really teach college students? Great!"

Or, "I've heard that the professor who is teaching this course is spacey — way-out (or weird or vague or difficult). I think I'm really going to need help. Do you teach any psychology courses?" (or math or whatever it is that the student needs).

If I believe that I can teach the course the student needs, I sure try to do it. I like to work with older persons because it is a nice change from working with grade school students. Older students like to spend a while talking about politics, community and world affairs, theater, and all the things that adults are involved in. With younger children, you hear mostly about sports or television or the latest hit records.

When college students come for tutoring, they and you know there is a limited amount of time to do the work. At the close of the semester, they must know the ideas, the concepts, formulas and everything that has been covered in order to receive a good grade on the final exam. That means they will ask you to clarify any misconceptions, explain hidden meanings, interpret problems and their solutions, and in general, make the course understandable for them.

So, during the first session, discuss the course and find out what they need from you. It may be that they just lack confidence, and if, after a few sessions of working together, you can show them that they can do the work, they will be able to do so alone or with minimal help. If they think that they need more extensive help, the best thing you can do for them is to make sure that at the end of each session, they clearly understand what you have been teaching and that they can restate all the concepts thoroughly.

Here is an example of what I mean:

> A problem in a statistics course concerns the people in a certain area. But which people? Make sure the student understands the definitions of those people. Do the statistics include the adults and children? Only the adults? The married people or the singles? And when your student does figure out which people to use, can he figure out the method used to determine the answer?

It's one thing to follow a professor's instruction. "There is a problem just like this one in the book," he might say. "It is done the same way."

Great! That makes the problem easy. But what if that same type of problem is on an exam and the student cannot use books to prompt his memory? Rote learning is all right sometimes. However, it doesn't always make for complete understanding. And, as a result, the student may do poorly on tests. So doesn't it make more sense to explain why the problem is done in the required manner and teach a person how to do it? Of course!

The old saw about the professor who is brilliant but cannot teach is so true. We've all had at least one. And with that, another tale...

I had a psychology professor in graduate school who taught advanced statistics. He could rattle off terms like "means" and "averages" without hesitation. He understood statistics like a cook understands spices. So, he decided to reproduce his lectures on paper and then sell them to use as the textbook for his course. Now that sounds harmless. But he wrote out his lectures on legal sized sheets of paper, and he wrote in a *very, very tiny* script. And then, to make things worse, he had the printer reduce that tiny script by 10 percent. Naturally, this reduced the size of the already minute script to almost nothingness. Therein lay our first problem; we could barely read the words.

The second problem involved our understanding the material. This professor spoke very rapidly — staccato — as he lectured. He understood the work. Why didn't we? And besides, wasn't it all in his $10 unreadable text?

Those of us who were naturally gifted in math and word problems managed to do the work. Needless to say, there were some students who needed tutors from the beginning of the course. We even had students repeating the class. And the clincher to all this? Before he even began his first lecture, this professor gave out the names of a few of his students from previous semesters who were now tutoring for his course! So much for my old professor!

If you have a student who needs help in courses that consist mainly of readings and lectures, make sure he has read the assigned material before he comes to your sessions. Otherwise you will be twiddling your thumbs while he catches up on his reading. This method also gives you the opportunity to see what his problem is:

comprehension and interpretation, making inferences, and/or simple reading errors.

John was a freshman taking a survey of history course. He was majoring in electronics and reading courses were not easy for him. On his first three essay exams, he failed miserably. One of the exams dealt with the Crusades and their effect on history. He had read the works assigned, following the Crusaders and their travels, but somehow failed to make the connections between events. He had a difficult time retaining anything he read.

"John," I said, "I'd like to show you a way I've found that helps when you have to read and remember a lot of subject material. It may seem that this method takes a extra time and is unnecessary, but really it works and *saves time* by making the material easier to understand and remember."

These are the steps as I showed them to John:

1. Find out what the chapter is about by skimming it. Read titles and subtitles. Look at the pictures and graphs and read their captions.

2. Read questions at the end of sections and at the end of chapters. They give you an idea of what to look for.

3. Read the material *for meaning only.* Do not take notes or underline.

4. Read the chapter again and *this time* underline and take notes. The reason for doing this during the second reading is that you now have a better idea of what is important.

5. Answer any printed questions as you go along.

6. Do the work at the end of the chapter. If you have any trouble with a question, reread that section.

I smiled as I said, "Try this method, John, and at our next session we'll see if it works for you."

When John returned, he had a much more confident look about him. He settled down to work immediately.

"I think it works," he grinned. "In fact, I know it does. Let me tell you the cause and effect of Columbus' discovery!"

And he began:

"Crusaders going to the Holy Land traveled great distances for the first time. On these travels, they learned of luxuries like spices, silks, dyes and precious stones. When they returned home, demand grew for these articles, so trading was greatly increased.

"Marco Polo, who had heard about the distant lands, traveled to India and China, and when he returned he wrote of his discoveries. Now all European nations wanted to go there to trade. But the Italians, who were already trading with the Arabians, controlled the Mediterranean, and it took too long to go by land across the continents and caravans couldn't bring back as much goods as ships could.

"Portugal was the country that discovered the route around Africa. Prince Henry loved the sea and kept sending his navy down the Western coast of Africa. Bartholomew Diaz rounded the tip of Africa and then Da Gama sailed the rest of the way to India and China. So now Portugal controlled the African route.

"Columbus was convinced the world was round, and when Isabella of Spain gave him money and ships to find a western route to the Far East, he discovered America instead. So the cause was the Crusades; the effect was the discovery of America."

I smiled. "Was that so hard, John?"
He shook his head.

"And did you find it interesting? I think it's fascinating."

He agreed. (Could he have done that just to appease me? I didn't know.) Of more importance, he had learned a new and effective way to study.

Remember, every student is different. Therefore, you may have to explain a concept three different ways to one particular person before he understands it. You may also have to explain that concept three different ways, to each of *three different students.*

Most college students are serious and will study. A few won't. You must decide if the ones who won't try or won't give you their attention are wasting both your time and theirs. Then you can accept or reject them as students.

But for those who really are serious, be sure to allow them the time they need. Be a thorough tutor! They'll tell their fellow students about you, and you'll get terrific free advertising.

☆   ☆   ☆

Adults, those persons out of school who come to you for help, are a courageous group. They recognize they have a problem, and they want to do something about it. They're ashamed or embarrassed that they can't read well, can't spell better, or can't do certain types of math.

But some people *think* about what they would like to do and they talk about it, but they never *do* anything about it. Others, the ones who call, are brave. They're really ready to move forward and learn.

A woman called whose voice sounded so strained on the phone. "I'm 38 years old, and I can't spell. I've been a file clerk for 20 years and I've always wanted to be a secretary. I don't know why I've waited so long to do anything, but I finally decided it was time to learn. Can you help me? Will you take a student my age?" A few days later, Carole, a tall willowy blonde, walked hesitantly into my office. "I feel foolish," she said, "but it's now or never!"

# High School Dropouts, College Students & Adults

I gave Carole a little quiz I had devised and found her spelling was on a 3rd or 4th grade level. So I gathered together all my books and worked out a whole program to teach her to spell correctly. Each week she learned about 20 difficult words, using them in sentences, definitions, and stories until she knew them well. She reviewed at home each night. And at each succeeding session, I not only tested her on previously assigned words, but I also gave her a new set of words. She was delighted with her progress, and we worked together for many months. When she left, her attitude had changed. She no longer walked hesitantly, and her voice was strong. I'm confident she succeeded in obtaining the promotion she wanted.

Jan had a good paying job with a fund-raising agency. She was a college graduate and was married to a lawyer. She wanted to take the LSAT (Law School Aptitude Test) but the algebra and geometry frightened her. Her husband, who had been a math teacher before becoming a lawyer, had tried to help her, but there was so much emotional involvement that Jan just couldn't learn when studying with him.

When she arrived, I discovered that she not only had problems with *high school* math, she was unable to do even fractions. So, once again, I set up a program and we started at that point.

Another caller was Mrs. Sullivan, who was 70 years old! Who says you can't teach an old dog new tricks!?

"I want to read better," she said, "It takes me forever to read a book, and I seem to forget what I've read when I get to the next page. Can you tell me what I do wrong?"

What Mrs. Sullivan did wrong was to read so slowly that she was only reading one word at a time; therefore, she lost any ideas or thoughts that were contained in phrases and sentences. And why did she read so slowly? She thought she'd remember the story longer!

So we worked on reading in phrases and, later on, in sentences. I timed her without letting her know what I was doing, and was she surprised when she saw how much faster she was beginning to read! Teaching her was fun because we talked about the past as well as the present, and I learned a lot from her.

Adults need constant reinforcement that they CAN accomplish their objectives. They have to be told that they're not too old, they're never too old. They like to hear the compliment that they are strong enough to admit they need help and then seek it. And they deserve all the credit you give them, too!

## Chapter Twelve

# Preparing Students for the College Entrance Exams

In the many years that I have been tutoring students for the Standard Achievement Tests (SATs) and American College Tests (ACTs), I have heard enough war stories about teachers to write several books. And the stories are always the same whether they come from public schools, private schools, or religious schools: inept and uncaring teachers and schools which care only about their ratings, not the young people who look to them for knowledge.

Of course, there are many teachers who are good, caring people. They know what the students will face when they take the tests, so as educators, they try to prepare their students as much as they can within the parameters of the curriculum and the amount of time they have. Unfortunately, in a school system, these teachers can only teach what they are hired to teach and often do not have the time to return to basics and instill the necessary foundations their students may need.

When tutoring my students individually for the SAT, I teach both English and math; for the ACT test I also teach science and grammar. For the first twenty years, I taught the SAT and ACT together. When I moved to Los Angeles, the ACT was relatively unknown. Kids only wanted classes for the SATs.

There are only eight students in each of my classes. Sixteen students arrive at the same time and then they are divided into two classes. They take a short SAT quiz in math and English so that I and the tutor who works for me can separate the faster kids into one group and the ones who need more time in the other. The reason I keep my classes to eight is so that we can give more personal attention to each student. With so few participants, we can usually see who is frowning, erasing a wrong answer, or pleased with what he or she is doing. Our students know they can ask as many questions as they need in order to understand our explanations. The students stay for three hours; they work on math and English for one and a half hours each.

At first I taught the verbal part of the tests because teaching English was more challenging than teaching math. Every math problem has an exact answer — even if it is one that says the problem cannot be solved. English can be ambiguous. Many vocabulary words have more than one meaning, and it's possible for students to interpret sentence completions and analogies differently. And many students don't read a great deal so they have trouble with reading comprehension in both tests.

The verbal portion of the SAT is quite different from that of the ACT. For the SAT, students need to know many vocabulary words, some of which they may not have heard before or would understand only within the context of a sentence. Can you imagine seeing an analogy that says "sheep: bleat :: as cow :_____"? Do most people really know that the "bah-h-h" that a sheep utters is called bleating and that the "moo" sound that a cow makes is called lowing? As I said before, many students have troubles with vocabulary words, and if they don't read much, they even have trouble with words that are considered common. There are students who do not know what a hangar is for or what an accomplice is — even when those words are used in analogies such as:

1.     pig: sty :: airplane: _____
2.     colleague: worker :: criminal: _____

The question asks if a pig is in a sty, where is an airplane? One of the choices and the correct one is "hangar." The next question asks if a colleague works with a worker, then who works with a criminal? One of the choices and the correct one is "accomplice."

Then there are sentence completions. A sentence is used in which a word or words are left out, and the student has to figure out which choices are the correct ones by finding the clues in the sentence. An example:

"Writing the Great American Novel is a difficult goal to achieve; it is as _____ as winning a 65 million dollar lottery."

**A**. chimerical  **b**. crucial  **c**. sporadic  **d**. cynical  **e**. superfluous.

Do *you* know? Did you find the clue? It is "a difficult goal to achieve." The answer is "a." How many students know that "chimerical" means elusive? My students learn to look at all the words first. If they know what four of them mean and those meanings don't fit the sentence, then they choose the word they don't know, in this case "chimerical," and that has to be the correct answer. They also learn that if they can eliminate three answers, they should take a chance and pick one of the remaining two choices.

And the reading comprehension? I am constantly appalled at how difficult that is for so many students! The English portion of the SAT and the reading part of the ACT contain several reading passages, and many students have trouble because they have not learned how to find a topic sentence. Those who don't read very much, tell me that they not only don't enjoy reading, they abhor it!

What happened to those enthusiastic first and second graders who couldn't wait to read? The ones who couldn't wait to get their own library cards? Some of that excitement came from home, but most of it came from school. But later, too many teachers made reading only a subject that had to be taught, not a pleasure that could be enjoyed for a lifetime. Why is it so hard to help children retain their curiosity and wonder and sense of adventure that comes from reading? Too many of our students lose that excitement and stop reading, and then when they face comprehension tests, they are in big trouble.

Today, teachers do not teach dates; they do not teach timelines; they teach ideas. That's fine until students are studying for the SAT history achievement test, and there is a question asking in which years the Civil War was fought and the kids don't know! The answer is 1861 through 1865, in the 19th century; oftentimes I have gotten answers like "Sometime in the 19th century." And when I say, "But there were 100 years in that century. What years are we talking about?" I get blank stares. Many of them confuse the Revolutionary War with the Civil War. Can you believe that a few of my students think Jefferson wrote the Declaration of Independence during the Civil War? Sometimes I get carried away with the sheer lunacy of it all and tell my students I'm glad that the War of 1812 had a number! But that doesn't matter anyway because they don't know what else was happening at that time.

The ACT has four sections: English, Reading, Math, and Science.

The science section is made up of seven science passages. Students have to be able to interpret data, graphs, charts and tables and then choose answers that best explain the information given. The test also may present an experiment with different viewpoints. Many of the test questions require just plain common sense. If students already know facts like "the temperature" is the answer to "What makes the difference between frost and dew?" that's terrific!

The English part of the ACT tests diction, grammar, punctuation, sentence structure, logic, style, and interpretation. Isn't all of that supposed to be part of the English curriculum from grade one to graduation? Then how come so many kids don't do well on the English section of the test? The kids have an awful time with grammar. Long before I coached for the entrance exams, I discovered that many high school English teachers do not consider English grammar very important to teach. Students say their teachers tell them to use a comma every time they pause, whether in a story, an essay, or on a term paper. Students separate subject phrases from verbs with a comma; they use commas in place of semicolons and colons. They sometimes don't even recognize the subjects or verbs. And if there is a prepositional phrase between the subject and verb, they really become confused.

Kids not only use too many commas, they do not know when to use colons, semicolons, when to use who and whom, etc. When I began coaching for the ACTs, I found that very few students did well on the grammar portion of the test. Out of a possible 33 (this was the high English score until fall, 1989; today it is 36) a great number of kids were getting in the low 20s. So I wrote a seven page pamphlet — writing the *rules* my way: simple and easy. A rule was followed by sentences showing right and wrong usage in English grammar. The following are some of them:

**COMMAS** are among the most commonly abused punctuation marks. The fewer commas you use, the better your grammar will be.

1. Use two commas or none between a subject and verb. If you use only one, you will be separating the subject from what is happening.

### WRONG

**A)** A baby girl named Josie, was born on Oct. 12. (Girl is the subject and was born is the verb.)

### CORRECT

**B)** A baby girl named Josie was born on Oct. 12.

**DANGLING MODIFIERS** (a gerundial or participial phrase). The phrase at the beginning of the sentence modifies the first noun following it.

**WRONG**

**A)**  Running down the street, the car hit the young man.

(The car was not running, the young man was.)

**CORRECT**

**B)**  Running down the street, the young man was hit by a car.

Defining a "dangling modifier" is hard; to put it in a few words is easier. So I will say, "After a phrase like 'Born during the Chicago snowstorm in 1967, ...' you must tell who or what was born."

I could have used the rules straight out of the English grammar books, but sometimes they are so confusing, it's hard for the kids to understand them.

My students laughingly called the pamphlets " Mrs. Shapiro's Easy English Rules" because they were so easy to learn.

The math section is made up of problems similar to those in math textbooks. If the students have done well in classes, they'll do well in this section. There are no deductive reasoning questions, just straight math. And yet, math is hard for many high school students. I had always assumed that all juniors, at least those in average or advanced classes, knew the basic facts of math: fractions, decimals, percentages, word problems, and averages. What a lesson I learned!

☆  ☆  ☆

Lennie was studying for the ACT and came for private lessons. He was a wonderful swimmer and a magnificent diver; he had courage, stamina, and was, overall, an outstanding athlete. What he wasn't was a math student. The ACT test begins with very simple problems. For example, there was one question in which Lennie had to simply divide fractions; he couldn't. Another question, a word problem, asked if a man bought a car for $900, paid 1/3 at the time of the sale, 1/2 of what he still owed 30 days later, and then the remaining balance in 60 days, how much was the remaining balance? Lennie didn't even know where to begin. I was stunned. I knew some juniors had trouble with geometry or algebra, but even the basics? I asked him what level math class he was in and he replied that he was in an average algebra class. Not a basic level class, you understand, but one step up — an average math class. How could that happen, I wondered, to get as far as algebra and not know fractions, so I asked him how his teacher felt about that. His answer? "My teacher said not to worry about it. I won't need to know fractions much in the future."

Betty was in a SAT class and having problems with math. She excelled in English. It was the fourth session and it was her turn to answer a math question on percents. She looked up timidly and said, "I never learned how to do percents or decimals. I can't do this."

Betty stayed after class; first we worked on decimals. She had never learned what the decimal points meant in a number: what did .45 mean? She had never learned that the first place after a decimal point represents tenths, then hundredths, thousandths, and so on. When she did learn that, she could read .45 as 45 hundredths. Then we worked on percents and what they mean. Betty learned to change percents to decimals and decimals to percents. The next week there was another problem using percentages, and Betty knew what to do.

I knew that I might run into students with problems like these now and then. But it happens again and again. My students say, "I don't understand why I have such trouble in math. I have a tutor who says I am doing great. I am getting high B's and A's in my homework and most of my tests, yet every time I take a final or practice tests for the college exams, I do poorly. I guess I'm just not good at math."

It is the job of tutors when they first encounter a student to find out what basic skills the student is lacking. It is the lack of those skills that make math hard for students. Yes, with help they can do their homework from day to day, but when it comes to a test and there is no one sitting next to them to help them, they freeze and do poorly. It is imperative that they learn those skills that all math is based on. And it can be done. It just takes time.

## Setting Up Classes

I had been coaching juniors individually for the entrance tests for about a year when two of my students asked me if I would consider teaching classes. They had mentioned my name to several of their friends and they all wanted to come together. The idea appealed to me so I began to study the competition.

At that time there wasn't a great deal of competition for classes in my area. There was one extremely well-known organization with offices nationwide. It was so large that it only needed a small ad in the newspapers to get a great number of students. When I called for information, I learned that there were 20 to 25 students in a class, the classes ran for ten to eleven weeks, and each one was 4 hours long. Their offices were open many hours of the day and evening, and students could come there to study with tapes written for the SATs. The teachers were often graduate students working for their master's degrees. The company wrote the materials that were used, and either students "rented" the materials or bought them for what seemed like a lot of money. I was able to obtain the material and when I read it, it seemed to me to be much more difficult and ambiguous than the actual SATs were. I was incredulous wondering how even an average student could understand much of it.

The other competitors were local ones; some had ten to fifteen students, one had eight, and the rest only taught individual students. At that time, no high schools offered classes. Every person I spoke with at these local organizations used materials published by companies like Arco, Barron's, and a few college textbook publishers who printed books to aid college-bound students. I believed that these books also went into depth beyond the requirements of the tests.

I wrote down all the information I had gathered and proceeded to figure out my plan. I liked the idea of eight students and three hour sessions. I also liked the short terms — seven to eight weeks. But I didn't like the books available. Luck was with me! I needed a certain book from an Eastern publisher, and when I opened its catalog, I noticed an ad for a book called 5 SATs. This book contained tests that had been given the previous year. I ordered one and found that I could order these books directly from the college board. If I ordered more than 50, I would get a discount. This made me wonder if I could order tests directly from the publishers of the ACT tests. I called their offices in Iowa and found that I could.

I had to figure out my costs before I could determine what I wanted to charge for classes. The very first time I advertised, there were only seven weeks left before the SATs and ACTs, so I decided to make this a trial test. I placed a one-eighth page display ad in our local suburban areas newspaper for two weeks, and I charged $150 for a five week course. I didn't expect much interest with such little notice so I was pleasantly surprised to sign up six students. And not only that: I discovered how much fun I had teaching these college tests and how much I enjoyed having a group of students. So I wanted more: several classes with eight students maximum in each. The question was how to beat the competition and how to make myself known to as many persons as I could.

My husband suggested I use direct mail and gave me the name of a friend who advised me to do a two-step mailing, starting four to five months before the actual start of my classes. The first step was to mail a letter together with a business reply card to the parents of all the juniors in my suburb and all the surrounding ones. If the parents were interested, they could either mail back the card with their names, addresses and phone numbers, asking for more information, or they could call me direct. The second step was to mail back my brochure, a registration form and a schedule sheet.

But first I had to get a mailing list. That was easy; most mailing houses do have lists of students. I went to an friend who was a commercial artist, and he designed my brochure. Then I went to a printer and got the costs for the letters and envelopes, cards, brochures, registration and schedule forms. I also had to know what the postage for all the mailings would come to and how much the books and paper supplies would be.

Armed with these figures, plus the salary for a teacher to work with me, I determined what I needed to charge for my classes in order to make a good profit.

In the fall of the year, I sent out 6000 letters. I wanted to fill six classes: three for the early spring tests, and three for the June tests. I had been told that a one percent return on my mailing would be very good. Imagine my excitement when I got a three and one half percent return! My classes filled almost immediately and many disappointed parents begged me to open a second class on Sundays. I already had classes scheduled for Sunday morning, Tuesday and Thursday evenings, so I added another class on Sunday afternoon.

The letters I sent were an added benefit to my private practice. In the letters I mentioned in a P.S. that I also did private tutoring. Because many students wanted to work individually, I increased my private practice workload by 50 percent. So now I not only had six filled classes with a total of 96 students but also 27 who came for private lessons. I was working hard; Saturday was my only free day, but I loved what I was doing!

My fees have gone up 400 percent in 27 years, but there is also much greater competition for classes and private tutoring. Several organizations have franchised across the country, and most of the high schools and junior colleges are now offering classes. Therefore, if you want to coach students for these exams, your advertising has to be powerful, and your teaching has to be par excellence.

There are a few drawbacks in teaching the same material — not only to a great many classes but also to your private students. It's easy to become bored, but luckily new students help alleviate that problem. Still I need a respite whenever I can get it. From the middle of June to the middle of August and again from the third week of December until school begins in January, I do not teach. I also take a spring break when schools take theirs. I've tried "retiring" twice. I tried it first in 1987. It lasted seven weeks. In the winter of 1991 when we moved to Los Angeles my retirement only lasted for three months! I guess teaching is in my blood.

It was 1984. During the years that I had been having classes, I was unhappy with all the books that were published to help students prepare for these tests. Some of the questions asked students to answer material they would never have to know or deal with. In the analogy sections, there were questions like this:

"INTERESTED: _____::

   **a.** passion: caring    **b.** bold: arduous
   **c.** fire: conflagration   **d.** fearless: intrepid
          **e.** penurious: money

What were these publishers asking for? There is never a blank in the original analogy. In some math sections the explanations used for correct answers didn't always give enough information or the information was confusing.

There were books that covered both the English and math portions of the test, and there were some that only covered one or the other. Because vocabulary is such an important part of the English section of the SAT, I looked for books with good vocabulary lists and definitions. Most English books or English sections of a book had a vocabulary list that contained at least 1000 words. There were even books on vocabulary alone that were called "SAT Word Lists; these books contained lists and definitions of words that were supposedly on the SAT tests.

I leafed through all the books looking for the best vocabulary list to use. As I checked each one, I saw that the lists were either too complex — they listed a myriad of words that had never been seen on an SAT — or they were too simplistic — they didn't contain enough words.

I had copies of many different SATs that had actually been given over the past years so I knew which words were important to know. There was no list that met my standards which was to define those words *actually* used on the test using only the definitions the SAT asked for, so I decided to write my own dictionary.

First, I called my daughter Suzie whom I and many others knew was extraordinary in everything she touched. She had a phenomenal vocabulary and knew all the shades of meanings of a word. I asked her if she would like to co-author the dictionary with me; I would choose the words (because I had access to all the SAT books) and she would write definitions and sentences to explain the definitions. I was elated when she said yes.

At that time there was a section of the test called opposites. A word was given in bold face, and students had to pick its opposite from the choices given. I made a 3x5 card for each word on the "opposites" section of the test. I also added words from the choices given. For example, from the opposites questions:

**1. CURSORY:**
   **a.** thorough **b.** flattering **c.** ostensible **d.** ludicrous
   **e.** amusement

**2. DIATRIBE:**
   **a.** commendation **b.** amusement **c.** containment
   **d.** erudition **e.** fluctuation

I made cards for cursory, ostensible, ludicrous, diatribe, containment and erudition. I copied words from sentence completion questions.

Contrary to their agreement, the investment company did not ask permission to sell the magnate's stock, thereby_____ the contract.
   **a.** rescinding **b.** inhibiting **c.** abrogating
   **d.** sanctioning **e.** vouchsafing

"C" is the correct choice. Many of my students didn't know several of the other choices so those words were also put on cards.

I alphabetized all of the cards and wrote the code number for the tests they were on. When a word was used more than once, I wrote all of the different test code numbers on the card. On the backs of the cards, I wrote the definitions that were called for on the SAT. In a regular dictionary the word "grate" has many meanings:

**(verb) 1.** to shred a potato; **2.** to grate on one's nerves, to irritate
**(Noun)1.** the grating over a sewer; **2.** hearth in the fireplace

The SAT tests only use the definition "to irritate," so we used that one.

Writing a dictionary is tedious work. My pile of cards grew higher and higher, and when I finally finished presorting the words, I checked to see which words were used most often. I found 810, so we titled our book, *The 810 Most Commonly Used Words on the SAT*. I mailed Suzie the words I had chosen, and she wrote the definitions using sentences that were interesting and clever and easy for anyone to understand. Some of the words and definitions read like this:

**BANE:** (noun) source of bad luck. Her evil stepmother was the bane of Cinderella's existence.

**LUDICROUS:** (adj) ridiculous. "Not having a pencil is a ludicrous excuse for not finishing your work," the teacher said.

The book was printed and each of my students received one with instructions to use it when they were doing their homework and came across a word they didn't recognize. I learned later that many of them used the book when they were doing their school homework! Most of my students used the book; a few of them even *memorized* it! I never assigned that task; they chose to do it themselves. Two of them told me later that memorizing the words helped them to get over 750 out of a possible 800 on the verbal portion of the test.

Every four years we update the book, adding new words and deleting others that haven't shown up very often in those intervening years.

For years, whether enrolled in classes or private sessions, I would give each of my students the *5 SATs* book, copies of three ACT tests, sheets with geometry theorems and algebra rules, the dictionary, and a folder to hold these items and the many more instructional sheets my teachers and I had written. I would tear the answer sheets out of the

SAT book and the ACTs for a very good reason: in my very first class, two of my students kept getting perfect scores on their homework. This didn't make sense. It's almost impossible to get 800s on both the math and English portions of the test, and when I would ask these students questions, they had difficulty answering them.

The other students in the class and I were puzzled until one of them asked quietly, "Are you two looking up the answers and just writing them in?"

The two conspirators grinned sheepishly. I had not torn the answers out of their books!

After that there were no answer pages left in books. If the kids can't do their homework, they circle the questions or problems to go over in class.

The College Board stopped printing the 5 SAT book in 1993 when they revised the test. They now print a book that is a study guide and includes several tests, some PSATs and some SATs. It is very expensive so I ask the students to purchase them for use in the classes.

The ACT company also stopped printing their tests. Now they are printed in a manner similar to the SAT books.

Our classes are very heterogeneous: the kids range from those in Learning Disability classes to those who rank #1. We divide the classes, putting the top half of the students in one group and the lower half in another. Sometimes, though, there is a problem. Some students are great in math and poor in English and vice versa, so the classes are more mixed. This, however, does not bother the kids. They want to learn so they work together and they get extra time when necessary.

In math some students forget geometry theorems and algebra rules, so we spell them out on paper. We teach students to use the easiest ways to do math. We insist they draw pictures — to work every problem out on paper. "No one," we say, "gets a blue ribbon for handing in a neat, clean test or doing the problems in his head. It's very easy to make a careless mistake and lose points unnecessarily."

For a problem like the following: $\frac{3a}{a} + \frac{1}{a} = 6$ students often forget to find a common denominator and even when they do, they forget that 6 is a whole number over 1 and needs to have that same common denominator.

We say repeatedly, "It's a timed test, so look at the problem closely to see if there is a clue to doing the work quickly. Do problems the easy, fast way. You are working against a clock. Fast and easy is the basic rule." For this next problem,

$$1 - (1-1/2)\ (1-1/3)\ (1-1/4)\dots\dots(1-1/16) =$$

we tell the kids to subtract the first few numbers in the parentheses and then note that the problem now reads 1 - (1/2) (2/3) (3/4) etc. and all they have to do is cancel out the 2s, 3s, 4s all the way through 15s. They end up with 1 - 1/16 and get 15/16.

After teaching the SATs for so many years, I recognize what kinds of problems are given and how often; therefore I can tell my students what they *must* learn and remember.

We are always delighted when we see kids picking up on these ideas. We illustrate our methods on paper and give them out to the kids who feel they need more help. We also help those who are the advanced math students. Dane, my math teacher, had gone through old SATs and made separate sets of worksheets with the harder problems for arithmetic, algebra, geometry, quantitative questions and logic. Several years later Sharon did the same with the ACTs. Those worksheets were so valuable that I still use them. By the time the classes are over, most of the students' folders are bulging!

No matter whom we are teaching, my private students or those in the classes, my teachers and I constantly ask questions and press our students to ask questions. "If you walk out of here feeling like you didn't get your questions answered or you don't understand the material we're working on, then you're cheating yourselves. We want you to learn, to understand, to feel that you know what you need to know at test time. And we have to feel we've done our best. So please ask questions, and if you don't want to ask in front of the class, come early or stay late. You're here to learn and we're here to teach."

We get through to most of the kids. There are always one or two who are too timid to speak up no matter how tactful we are; and naturally there are also a few who are too cocky to want to appear puzzled in front of their classmates.

Parents and students feel that we do a good job. Many parents have sent two or three of their children to us. They have recommended us highly and have said we could use their names as references.

I had been tutoring for these tests for several years when Mrs. Keats, the mother of one of my junior high students, told me she was starting a software company for computers, and one section of it was to be educational. She had already hired someone to write a disk for students to use when studying for the United States Constitution test. She asked me to author disks for both the English and math sections of the SAT test. At first I balked. Did I really feel I could write in the same manner as those who drafted the SAT test? I knew I was familiar enough with the SAT itself.

After a few weeks, I decided that this was something I would like to do. Mrs. Keats gave me a contract and the name of the programmer. I contacted a well-known lawyer-author who made sure my contract protected me. Writing the material was easy; making sure it worked with the program was not. I wrote the material so that the correct answers explained why they were right and all the wrong answers stated why they were wrong. The questions got progressively harder just as they do on the actual SAT tests. I needed hundreds of questions to fit on each disk and I spent a lot of time composing them.

Eventually I wrote two English disks and one math disk that were sold across the country. Just as I finished the second math disk, the company went bankrupt. Until that time, I had enjoyed collecting all the magazines that had full page ads for my disks, but I had even greater fun when I visited stores in many cities and saw disks with my name on them displayed on the counters. A few of the managers even asked me to autograph some copies!

Teaching ACT/SAT classes is fun. The majority of the kids are great, witty, and a joy to teach. One Sunday morning during class, a few of the eight kids were grumbling, but with a lilt in their voices. "We're tired! It's 9:00 on a Sunday and we got in late last night! We should be sleeping."

I laughed and asked if I should make coffee every week to keep them on their toes. Eight faces lit up. "Would you? Wow, that would be great! Would you do it every week? Could we bring doughnuts to go with it?"

I agreed to serving coffee during class and the food during the break but only on the condition that they would work very hard during class time. They promised. The next week I made an urn of decaffeinated coffee. The kids who drank it were ecstatic! "Does this ever make a difference! I'm really wide awake!"

The coffee was on the table each week until the end of the sessions, and every week the kids remarked how alert they were. I never did tell them it was decaffeinated.

One year my birthday fell on a class day. I wanted to go out to dinner to celebrate but couldn't. At the break, the lights went out and in marched my husband with a birthday cake complete with candles and large enough to serve all of my students and the two of us.

Later on in the year, one of my students wanted to celebrate his birthday. He not only brought cupcakes, but cokes, colored napkins and candy. We sang, laughed, and got more work done than in previous sessions.

During Homecoming season kids talk about their schools' football games and parties. During Prom time, they talk about dresses, tuxes and dinner plans.

## Problems That Can Occur

Teaching students in classes also has a serious side. During classes I always ask my students if any of them is having problems with the work, my explanations, etc. and most of those who are will say so.

Not Pete. He sat very quietly, erasing wrong answers and writing in my explanations. The only time he spoke was when I asked him for an answer. I watched his face closely, as I did the others, to see if I could read any of his expressions, but I couldn't. I was so troubled that one day I asked Pete to stay after class. And then I got my answers.

A prestigious university had offered Pete a hockey scholarship, one which he needed for monetary reasons. He wanted desperately to go to this school but his parents alone couldn't afford the fees. He had taken the ACT once before and scored an 18. He needed to raise that score by at least 4 to a 22.

"I like the classes and I'm learning a lot, but there are times when I don't understand your explanations. Sometimes I interpret words and sentences differently, yet I still get correct answers."

"Uh-Oh." I mentally lambasted myself. "What have you done? How many other kids feel like Pete does? Should I ask and leave myself open to more criticism? And yet that's how I'll improve — by input that's constructive. Darn it, why haven't I been more observant and more attentive? Why was I so complacent?"

I looked at Pete. "Will you show me what you're referring to 'cause if you're getting the right answers, then what you're doing may make sense." I looked at his work and saw what he meant. People do see things differently, and I needed to know that.

My son David once said, "You only learn from mistakes, Mom." How right he was! From that time on, I always ask if someone in my classes has solved a problem or answered a question in a different way, and if so, would he or she mind explaining that method to the class? Perhaps another student might understand that method or idea better than mine. I have heard some weird suggestions and ideas over the years, but if they work, and other students can understand them, that's fine.

Incidentally Pete did very well and got his scholarship. Pete's problem wasn't the only one I encountered. Fern was a big believer in teenage "chic." Her style of dress had a very trendy quality, no doubt about it. Once she came to class wearing her Michael Jackson outfit: one glove and sunglasses. Another time she wore a sweatshirt draped over one shoulder full of different sized holes she had cut into it. She had dyed a part of her hair orange. It got so that every week we all looked forward to her arrival with baited breath — anticipating what Fern would be wearing and how she would look. Fern didn't want to be in class; she wanted to be anywhere else having a fun time.

Fern didn't show up for our third class session and so did not receive the material I passed out for the following week. Believing that she would appreciate my thoughtfulness, I mailed the material to her home. A week later, she stormed into my office.

"How dare you!" she shrieked. "How could you!?"

I looked at her blankly. What did I do?

"My mother opened the package you mailed to me," Fern fumed, "and knew immediately I had skipped class last week. She was so angry that she grounded me for a month!" She paused and then continued ranting. "Don't you ever do that again!"

Needless to say, although Fern came to the rest of the classes, she never spoke to me again.

From that time on, I only mailed out material when a student or parent called to request it.

Denise didn't like classes either, and she never did any of the work. Once, during a winter class session, I mailed letters in plain envelopes to the parents of my students. The letters stated that we had now reached the half-way mark in our sessions and that they might want to ask their children how they were doing in class: did they understand the work and could they do it? I did this hoping that the parents would see for themselves how things were going. Some parents called to say they were impressed. Others did differently.

About six weeks after the SAT test date, Denise's mother called, and she was furious! "Denise's SAT test score was 90 points lower than her PSAT score, and it's all your fault!"

I remembered the letters I had sent out to the parents, and I asked her if she had received hers.

"I sure did. I went into her room and saw all of the test books on her desk. I asked Denise if she was doing all of the work you assigned and if she understood it, and she said she was all caught up and doing just fine."

"That's interesting," I replied. "Denise never came to class with her homework done. I know because when I asked her for answers to any questions, she didn't have them. It appeared as if she was copying the work in class." I tried to defend myself but to no avail. I had never before had any parents blame me for their children's scores.

Denise's mother kept carping. Finally I wised up and put an end to the call, but I couldn't shake the hurt I felt. What did I do wrong, and what could I have done better? Over 6000 students have been in my classes and that has only happened to me about three times. The odds are in my favor.

☆  ☆  ☆

Generally speaking, it is easier to become close to private students because we are alone for the sessions. My students feel free to talk about themselves because they know that anything they tell me will be strictly confidential. Such was the case of Mia, a pretty, petite and quiet girl. She was of average intelligence, and though she worked very hard, much of the material on the SAT was difficult for her. During the hours that we were together, she would work on the test and then spend a few minutes talking about her social life and how great it was.

But each week I could see Mia become more tense, and as the date for the test grew closer, I could sense Mia slowly withdrawing from me. Several times I asked her what was wrong, but she wouldn't tell me. I could tell she was afraid to say anything.

Then one day she finally broke down. Within her Korean community was a girl named Lee who was her own age and who studied until one or two in the morning seven nights a week. Lee was tied for valedictorian, and many of the parents in the community pressured their children to emulate her. The kids themselves didn't want to be like her because she had no social life and was a loner.

I knew all of this was true because Lee, who was in one of my classes, told me she needed a total of 1500 or more on the SAT. She wanted to be accepted into a prestigious university which had a six year medical school program for very bright students. On Sundays Lee and several other students came directly from the same church to my classes and yet Lee always sat alone. She had no time for friends so the others spared no time for her.

"I'm not like her," Mia cried. "Why can't my parents see that?" She was miserable.

I tried to reassure her, but no amount of encouragement helped, and I felt powerless as I watched her become more anxious and fearful.

The test date arrived. On each of the test dates, I wake up early and think about my students throughout the morning. On this day, I thought especially about Mia. About 1:00 that afternoon, she called me. "It was tough," she reported, "but I did the best I could. I hope it was good enough."

I reminded her that she could take the test again, but that didn't matter to her. *This* test score did.

About five weeks later, I got a call — from a hysterical girl and extremely angry parents. "Mia got an 870 on her test!" They were enraged. "She let us down! How could she do that?" How could they, a well known physician and his socially prominent wife, live down their daughter's terrible score? They were livid. Mia kept crying.

After listening for what seemed forever, I broke in and suggested that Mia and her parents talk to each other, that they let Mia explain the terrible pressure she felt from them. "If you agree, I'd like to be with Mia when you talk together. She may need some support and I really know the whole situation." There was a strained silence and then they agreed.

We had our meeting. Two months later, Mia retook the exam and this time I did not hear from her or her parents.

Two years later, I was in a department store when I felt a tap on my arm. I turned and there was a smiling Mia, standing with her mother. I reached out to her, saying, "Mia, you look wonderful! What are you doing now?"

She laughed, a tinkling, happy laugh. "I'm at the university. I'm an arts major and I love it!"

☆　☆　☆

That summer I had a private student from the same Korean community. Jan was bright and a fast learner. Every hour with her was a pleasure. She asked insightful questions and absorbed knowledge quickly and easily. Jan couldn't wait until the test was over: the Monday following the test she would be leaving for a two week trip to France. She was confident and felt sure that she would do very well on the test. She was very unconcerned — until a week before the test. That day she came to my office, her face swollen from crying. "My mother says I have to get at least a 1350 on the SAT or I can't go to France!"

It was like a bombshell had exploded. "I wonder," I said quietly, "if your mother realizes the kind of pressure she's putting on you?"

"No," she wailed. "She doesn't care!"

I felt that I had to do something. I felt sure that Jan would score at least a 1300; she almost always scored perfectly on her SAT homework.

"Would you like me to call your mother?"

"Oh, yes. Please."

After she left, I called her home and told her mother how hard her daughter was working, how very bright she was, and that too much pressure might make Jan panic and make careless errors. "Please encourage her," I pleaded. "If she knows that you love her no matter what she scores, she'll relax and do extremely well."

When Jan came for her next session, she threw her arms around me. "Mom loves me! For me! She said I should go in Saturday, take the test, and then come home and pack for my trip! I'm going to Paris! I'm really going!" It was good to see her relaxed, all the tension gone.

Six weeks later, Jan called me. "I had a wonderful time in Paris, and to top it off, I got my scores in today's mail and guess what? I got a 1380! 680 in English and 700 in math. Can you believe it?"

I could and did. With such supportive parents, Jan would do well in anything.

David had trouble with his eyes. He had difficulty reading the small print in textbooks, newspapers, and other printed materials; therefore, he had always had difficulty in school and had to work very hard to maintain good grades. David wanted to go to college and become an engineer, but he was concerned about taking the ACT test. He went to his college guidance counselor who advised him to forget about college. Taking the ACT would be impossible. How could he see the print well enough to read the test?

Fortunately, David had a caring ophthalmologist who called an administrator at the central ACT offices. The doctor explained David's problem and asked what this executive could do to help his patient.

After hearing the predicament David was in, the administrator told the doctor that he would allow David to not only take an enlarged version of the ACT but also take it untimed. David was grateful, but he needed to study for the test and no one seemed to know how to overcome his problem.

David's mother called me and asked if I could help her son. I knew that I could if I had the right materials, so I said yes and we set up an appointment.

When it comes to printing, I ask my husband for help because that is one of the many things he knows well. "How do I solve this one?" I asked.

"Simple. Just take a few of the practice ACT tests you have and have the print blown up four times over." It was the perfect answer and it worked like a charm. David was able to read the tests easily and he went into the test with confidence.

I didn't hear from David or his mother for two years. Then one day she called me. It was time for her younger daughter to take the test. She remembered how well David and I had worked together and so pulled out my card which she had saved all that time.

"Oh, Eileen," she exclaimed, "David did so well on his test that there was no way I was going to call anyone but you. I kept your card and took a chance that you were still coaching kids for the tests."

I was, so we scheduled Leslie in for several appointments. Then she took a deep breath, and her voice grew more and more excited as she told me how well her son was doing in college. "He's in the first semester of his sophomore year, and getting high Bs and a few As in engineering school. Bless you, Eileen. We'll never forget you."

That conversation was one of the most rewarding ones I've had in my 27 years of tutoring.

In the early '90s we moved to the Los Angeles area. I had thought of retiring but I missed the kids so I decided to at least teach SAT classes. In California the ACT was just beginning to become known so few kids took it.

I found the attitudes here very different from those in Chicago. There students said that they would prepare themselves very well before their first SAT and ACT so that they wouldn't have to take it twice. If they weren't happy with their scores, *then* they would say they'd try it again. Here in Los Angeles it was common to hear, "I'm taking the SAT twice. If I don't do well, I'll take it a third time."

In Chicago, every student strove for at least an 1150 on the SAT. Most of them wanted very high scores so that they could go to Ivy League schools in the East, the highly ranked universities like UCLA, USC, Stanford, Northwestern, Emory in Atlanta, and some of the Big Ten schools. I do hear that here in Los Angeles too, but there are too many who say if they get 1000, they'll be happy. They talk about junior colleges.

Because a number of students who have immigrated to this area are in *basic* English classes, some counselors are saying these students cannot take SAT; they must be in *higher level* English classes. Because anyone can take the SAT—sixth graders, seniors, foreigners — I personally believe the counselors are afraid their students may do poorly and reflect on their school.

Michal was from Armenia and spoke English well. He came to my classes to prepare for the SAT. After a few weeks, he walked in extremely upset. "My counselor says I cannot take the SAT. The English classes I am in are too basic, and she won't give me the registration forms." My daughter, who was teaching the English portion of the SAT, and I were astounded!

"Anyone can take the SAT, Michal. Don't worry. We'll get you some forms." I got them from another school. Michal took the test and did well. He was very grateful and gave me a gift of Russian nesting dolls that his family had brought to this country.

Michal wanted to go to the California State University at Northridge. He spoke with his counselor who this time said, "The school won't admit you so don't bother to send in an application."

Suzie and I were really angry. "You go ahead and send it in. She can't keep you from trying."

So Michal mailed his application and was accepted. This time he brought each of us a huge bouquet of flowers.

A few years later his sister came to prepare for the SAT. Michal, she said, was preparing to go into premed. I hoped his counselor knew this.

☆ ☆ ☆

It's stories like this that make all tutors happy; they know they can help many students in many different ways.

## Chapter Thirteen

# Working With Parents

Parents, like kids, come in all sizes and shapes and with their own ideas about tutoring. Some are terrific to work with and some are not, but you can't do without them, so here are some tips I have picked up along the way.

When you first meet parents, you must decide what kind of parents you are dealing with. Most parents care a great deal about their children's educational progress...for a variety of reasons. Some parents want their children to learn as much as they possibly can so that they can be successful after their schooling is finished.

Some parents bring children who are gifted scholars and who are: one, bored in school or two, eager to learn more than they are learning in school. Pradeep was one of the latter; he was a very intelligent 6th grader and eager to learn. His parents encouraged him and although both of them were doctors and worked long and erratic hours, they managed to bring Pradeep every week at his scheduled time.

Some parents want their children to do well because they consider their children a reflection or extension of themselves and so those children must always be proving themselves to the parents. One father who was in his forties, and whom I'll never forget, brought his 17-year-old to study for the college entrance exams in one of my groups. This man made a point of showing all of us that he still carried *his* SAT score in his wallet because it was fairly high. Can you imagine what pressure his son lived under?

There are parents who feel their children are not getting a good enough education in school and therefore seek outside help. Remember Nancy (chapter 2) who had trouble in math, and Cheryl, whose teachers couldn't figure out what her problem was?

There are those who feel their children are mislabeled. Many of those kids are in Special Ed or in learning disabilities classes. Some others are those who have been held back a year or two; they often mature a little later and so are working at less than their full potential.

And there are always a few parents who just want their kids to do okay in school so they won't have to be bothered with them.

Parents bring their children to you because their emotional involvement makes it difficult for them to help their children. Or maybe they don't feel adequate in the subject material. For whatever reasons, they bring their kids.

When parents are too emotionally involved to help their children, I tell them not to try. "Just love your kids; show them you want to help and support them in every way possible. Leave the teaching and remonstrations, if there need to be any about schoolwork, to me. Because you have an emotional involvement, it is easier for me to cut through these kinds of problems."

I use analogies a lot when I talk to parents. For example: Marty's father is an accountant and Marty was having problems in math. His dad sat down and tried to explain the problem. After all, who knew math better? But Dad explained it at a level so far above Marty's comprehension that the work became even more confusing. His dad would say," It's so easy. Why don't you get it?" and Marty would become very upset.

Or take Mrs. Merritt who was a whiz in English when she was in school, and now *her* child, Gina, was having problems in comprehension and grammar! How could that be? So Mrs. Merritt tried to show her child how to do grammar, but lost her cool when Gina took too long to understand. Before they knew what was happening, both of them were emotionally tied up in knots. Everyone was angry. When this happens, there is no way a child is going to be receptive to any learning. "Just love your child," I repeat. "That's what parents are for."

The children who have to prove themselves usually have parents who also will tell you how to teach and what to teach. They want to be in control of the entire situation. They will break appointments at the very last minute, or they will call you too often and talk for too long. I once had a neighbor who sent her daughter to me. Brenda's mother felt that because we were friends, she could blame me for all of Brenda's school problems. Why didn't I call her teachers every time she spoke back to them (which was quite often!) and tell them I felt Brenda was right and they just weren't seeing things from Brenda's perspective? Or how could I be teaching fractions when her child was already in algebra and fractions was a fourth or fifth grade subject? Luckily there are very few of these parents.

There are other types of parents: those who say teachers are always right and their child is always wrong; those who call teachers, get no reaction so go to the principal who also doesn't help...now they want you to go speak for them; and those who bring their kids for tutoring, drop them off, and then have little to do with their children until report card time.

I had a student, Tony, the middle son of three boys, whose mother was a successful travel agent. She and her husband had done so well in their businesses that they could travel at any time to any place. They had a maid who took care of the kids and the house. Tony's older brother could do no wrong. Genius, she kept telling me. His younger brother was the baby...a precious child! Poor Tony...he couldn't do anything right! They felt they were doing everything they could for him by bringing him to me for help in school. Well, you know the old adage: "You can lead a horse to water but you can't make him drink."

# Working With Parents

To show his anger, Tony fooled around in school, did very little homework and so got D's and F's on his report card. I could always tell when report card time came. His mother would come to my office and instead of just dropping Tony off, there would be such a tirade that whoever was with me in the office would cringe. She would tell Tony that he was grounded for weeks, that she would pull him out of school and find a school for delinquents, and that she was just plain fed up with him. There was such tension in the air, you could touch it. Tony just became more sullen and I began to notice that although he used to come in dressed neatly, he now looked grubby and dirty. It seemed no one in the family even noticed.

This went on for two years until one night his parents came home, found his door locked and smoke coming out from under the door. He had fallen asleep in his bed, smoking a cigarette and drinking a can of beer. *Finally* they took notice and found a wonderful school for Tony to go to until he graduated. The administration there helped turn him around and he went on to college for a degree in engineering. But what he had to go through to be noticed!

☆ ☆ ☆

You must be firm with all the parents of your students. You must set parameters: you will talk on the phone for only a specified amount of time, you will need at least 24 hours notice of cancellation, and **you** will decide how to teach their children. If they are unwilling to abide by your methods and rules, then you have the choice of teaching or not teaching their children. Sometimes I run into difficulties because I enjoy working with some of the kids so much that I often don't act quickly enough to remedy uncomfortable situations. If the situations become too untenable, I tell the parents that it might be easier on the children if they take them to someone else.

The parents who don't want to be bothered about anything that happens in your office actually make tutoring easier. They think they have done their job by just bringing their children. The rest is up to you. You don't have to answer to them very often. Occasionally, they'll ask how their children are doing. It can sometimes be exasperating when you ask the parent to do something like help with a schedule and they don't. Or, you ask them to see that their children have new notebooks, and they are too busy to remember. Brush the frustrations aside. Helping the children is all that matters.

Parents who think their children are mislabeled often have a legitimate reason to be angry because their children have been placed in the wrong classes. If you decide to teach their children, you must be prepared to listen to the parents' frustrations, to listen to the bitterness they feel. The extent to which you help is up to you. If you think that the parents are right, be prepared for an onslaught of calls between them and you and between the teachers and you.

If the parents know you want to help, they may assume that they can call you as often as they want just to vent their feelings. Learn to limit your time. These parents are well-meaning, but sometimes forget that you have other students and obligations.

On the whole, parents who bring their kids to you do so for the sake of their children. They understand when you ask them to do something for their child; they will be on time for the appointments; they'll usually talk to you before they talk to teachers.

They are paying you, so be a good listener, but don't forget to draw boundaries on time.

Most of all, remember you are a good instructor and you know your job. Show self-confidence and understanding. The parents will respect you for it.

## Chapter Fourteen

# When Students "Graduate" — Saying Goodbye

"Goodbye and good luck. You'll do great."

Those few words shake me up more than any other words I know. They produce feelings of excitement that my students have become self-confident and secure enough to be on their own; they elicit feelings of my own self-worth that I have done a good job; they bring about a feeling of contentment that I have helped my students over some rough spots in their lives.

But those words also create a sense of loss. I become so close to my students, listening to their "ups and downs," seeing them on good days and bad, that when the time comes for them to leave, to "graduate" from tutoring, I feel a bittersweet separation.

Some of my students come for several years and some come for a few months, but no matter what the amount of time, they become my friends. And though I am very proud of them and eager for them to make their way in the world, it's wrenching to see them go.

I once thought these feelings were mine alone until I began noticing how many of my students lingered for one reason or another. We would agree that they were ready to be on their own without me. They were ready to go back to school, understanding all the things that had confused them earlier. Then I would hear remarks like, "I need to make sure I can do the work alone. Would you give me a quiz next week so that I can see I'm ready?" or "But there's this little area where I need help!" or "Can I see or call you to make sure I'm keeping up?" or "I think I'll take the college exam one more time, so can I come back for a few weeks before the test to brush up?" and those few sessions would become a month or more. I've even had kids drop by my offices just to say "hi."

I asked these kids several times if they were scared of being on their own, and they usually replied, "Oh, no. We can do the work, but we have enjoyed being with you so much."

I liked it too! I watched Ben grow from a small 5th grader into a six-foot-tall 8th grader. I watched Cheryl grow from a shy, introverted little child into a happy, outgoing young girl who did become a teacher. I saw Kim change from a disheveled, restless adolescent into a lovely young woman. I met her on the street one day and learned that she was happily married and had a year-old son.

I often wonder how my students are and what they're doing. What do they look like now? Children change so much as they grow up. Yet I try to make a clean break. I don't call the kids to see how they're doing. But I sure think about them. It's hard to believe that some are now parents who have children who could be old enough to be in high school themselves!

I tell myself that someday, I hope, I'll see their names or their pictures somewhere and then I'll know they're doing fine.

And for me, that will be enough..

# SECTION II

# The Business Side of Tutoring

Chapter Fifteen

# Qualifications

## Is Having a Teaching Certificate a Prerequisite?

Having a teaching certificate is obviously a plus. It tends to reassure the parents who ask about your credentials. It also helps when you talk to the school teachers about your students. The teaching certificate itself does not always make a tutor wiser or better at teaching, but it does show that you have had experience in the field. And to some parents, that may be the only qualification they care about.

On the other hand, you do not require a teaching certificate to tutor. Most parents don't have one, and they teach their children every day! Sisters and brothers and friends help each other without a teaching degree. So if you love to teach and enjoy watching others learn, and if you know a subject thoroughly enough to impart that knowledge to others, then you can tutor.

I once had a student who had come for help in math. One day she mentioned that she fallen far behind in French. I couldn't help her with that, but my daughter Suzie, a college student who excelled in French, could. She began working with Lauren and they worked well together. In a matter of weeks, Lauren was beginning to catch up and in a few months was getting above average grades.

A few years later, when I decided to write a dictionary for my SAT students, Suzie was my co-author. She had a knowledge of words that was incredible. She knew every nuance and when certain words *seemed* to be perfect for a sentence, she would say, "There's a shade of meaning to that word that doesn't work. Use this one instead." And she was always right.

In my SAT/ACT classes there are 16 students, eight of whom are studying math in my office, because the whiteboard is there to write on, while the other eight are in my family room working on English. Because of this arrangement, I always hire another teacher to work with me.

When I first began teaching these classes, I hired a certified teacher with a math degree. She was adequate but taught by the book. She was not innovative, inspiring or caring. Without any warning and after sixty-four students had signed up for four different classes, she informed me that her husband was transferred and she would not be able to teach with me. I was forced to advertise. My ad read:

> **PART-TIME:** High school math tutor. Immediate opening. Qualified, knowledgeable, innovative. Work Sundays and evenings. Send resume to _____.

I was in California helping my daughter, Suzie, with my new grandson when the resumes arrived at my home. A few days later my husband called me very excited. "I think I've got the perfect person for you. He is not a math teacher. His degree is in political science, but while he was at Swarthmore, he also studied at Wharton School of Business. I talked to him, and he's everything you want. He's exciting to talk to and when you hear everything he's done, you'll know how inspiring he must be. Can I make an appointment for the two of you?"

I'll admit I had reservations but decided to put them on hold until I interviewed Dane. And am I pleased that I did. Dane was only 23 years old but had wonderful references. He had held a myriad of jobs: he had tutored for the college entrance exams while in college, he had done copywriting, retail sales and telephone marketing. During our interview,

# Qualifications

I noted that he was very skilled at communicating ideas. He understood my needs and he presented himself superbly. He loved teaching and someday wanted to become a college professor, but for now he was trying several other options.

As I spoke with Dane, two things began to worry me. He was young and he was very good looking. Would the students pay attention to him and look up to him and would his good looks interfere with the girls' learning?

I asked Dane to sit in and teach a class. He was superb! He showed the kids the textbook method for solving problems but felt that for many math problems, there was an easier and faster way to do them. And so he would teach those methods. He constantly stressed the short amount of time allotted for the tests and why solving problems quickly was important. His enthusiasm was infectious, and my students loved him. I hired him on the spot. After he began teaching regularly, he often stayed after class to help kids who were puzzled. And if the kids were only able to talk to him before classes, he came early.

Dane was a runner. In college he was a three time qualifier for the NCAA Cross Country Championships and he had led his school team to victory in his senior year. After he started working with me, he would sometimes run several miles from his home to my office and then change clothing there. The students loved it; they felt he truly understood them and with the combination of Dane's being a young teacher and my being older, we really covered all the bases for the kids. We were a terrific team!

Dane stayed with me for three years, and when he "retired," he left a big hole. I hired other teachers but it took me two years to find another teacher as good as he.

For the next two years I hired certified math teachers. They were so bound up with teaching "right from the book," that quick and easy learning meant nothing to them. The kids had to know the "correct" way to do the problems, no ifs, ands, or buts. These people were extremely knowledge-able; they knew their work. They just didn't understand how to work with students studying for the college entrance exams.

I was feeling very frustrated the following year when I opened a resume from Sharon. She, like Dane, was not a math teacher; her degree was in actuarial accounting. But on her resume she wrote that she had tutored many high school students in all areas of math. Sharon had young children of her own, and I wondered if she would be able to teach on Sundays and evenings. But then I read her covering letter which stated those hours were just perfect, so I asked Sharon to come for a meeting and I discovered another great "teacher" like Dane.

Years later my husband and I moved to Los Angeles where I continued teaching SAT classes. I needed another teacher and I had no problem finding the most perfect one. My daughter, who now had five children of her own, said she would love to teach the English section of the SAT. Suzie did not have a teacher's degree but she knew English and was a wonderful teacher. She made learning fun for the students. She made them want to learn and they did. Their scores were always great. She loved the kids, and they loved her. I could always hear them laughing while they worked. And when class was over, they would stay behind to talk with her.

It is true, Suzie, Dane, and Sharon did not have teachers' degrees, but they knew their subjects, loved teaching and cared about the kids, and all of that showed in their performances.

## Chapter Sixteen

# T<sub>h</sub>e Business En<sub>d</sub> o<sub>f</sub> It

W hether tutoring is a part-time or full time business, there are some details to check out.

Many communities require that all businesses have licenses. If you live in a restricted residential area, you may have to determine whether there is a variance to tutor out of your home. Some communities allow tutoring if you are teaching a single student at a time. Some also allow you to have very small classes (5 to 8 students). You can find out this information at your city hall.

Check the insurance on your home. Make sure it covers anything that may happen to your students while they are on your property.

You may decide to incorporate. Learn how much that costs and learn about income taxes. There are many tutors who feel that it isn't cost effective to incorporate and so consider themselves "sole proprietors." Either way you have to keep track of your expenses and income. And having a separate banking account is a great help.

## Banking

If you have only a few students, you can use your regular checking account, *but* you must keep track of everything the same as if you have many students. Keeping the business in your own name makes it easier to use your regular account. If you decide to create a new business name, you first need to file a DBA (Doing Business As) statement which must be published in a local newspaper. When you go to the newspaper offices, ask the cost of publishing your statement and how many times it must be published. Be aware that newspapers charge differently;

usually smaller newspapers charge less than the larger ones.

Your statement must be made public for two reasons: the first is to make sure that no one else is using the name you have chosen. If your business name is original, then the second reason is to ensure that no one else can copy your name. When you get the papers in the mail saying your DBA statement has been approved, you can go to your bank and open an account in your new business name. Only your business income will go into this account and all your business expenses will be written by check and deducted from your business account.

## Expenses

Where you locate your business makes a difference. If you work out of your home and have an office there or use a certain area *exclusively* for tutoring, you can deduct that percentage of your home for income taxes. Save your bills for water, gas, electricity, house insurance, the part of your phone bill that pertains to your business, and all the repair bills to maintain your house. You can deduct the same percentage of these bills for income taxes. If you have an office outside of your home, keep your rent and phone bills, gas receipts and mileage records.

Other expenses that are tax deductible are advertising, stationery, printing (like brochures), and postage. If you drive to your students' homes, or if you visit schools, keep records; a percentage of your gas bills, maintenance on the car, and car insurance is deductible. The list goes on: publications you subscribe to that pertain to the business; fees for the professional societies you belong to; ongoing education classes or seminars you attend, your bank fees, and business gifts. You can deduct all of your travel expenses which are for business: plane and train fares, meals, and hotels.

Supplies include everything you buy for your business. Those include books, direct mail lists, copies you make, and all stationery supplies.

## Income

To make your life easier, tell parents that you would like them to pay you each time you see their students. Then there are no books to keep. You can also apply to your bank for a credit card processing arrangement. You can buy or rent the machine; the bank will charge you a small percentage of each payment made on it. Remember: bank charges differ, so shop around.

If parents ask you to change your usual fee arrangements, like paying every two weeks or every month instead of every session, make sure you have them sign a payment form. There are always a few people, whose children have seen you for several weeks, who will hold back on the money owed you and some may decide their child didn't do as well as they wanted them to and not want to pay at all. That is totally unfair because you have given your time to their child.

Doctors, lawyers and other professionals who have seen their patients or clients, send bills for their time and expect to be paid. You are a professional too.

A place to tutor (in or out of your home), how to set your fees and time schedules, advertising and other important areas are covered in other chapters.

## Chapter Seventeen

# Choosing Your Market

Tutoring others may be just the answer to your needs. But you may also have questions that need to be addressed such as:

"Just how large is the market for tutoring?" "Where do these students come from?" "Who are these students?" Let's take them one at a time.

## How Large Is the Market for Tutoring?

Very large. I started tutoring just as a lark to keep myself busy. My youngest child was in elementary school and coming home for lunch, so I wasn't ready to leave the house to go to work. I set up a classroom in my recreation room. I had some school books that my older children had used, I bought paper and pencils, and I put a classified ad in the local newspaper. Little did I dream that in less than two years my practice would grow so large that I would decide to move out of my recreation room into an office building.

## Where Do These Students Come From?

From everywhere! They come in all sizes, shapes, and ages. If they (or their parents) think you have the qualifications they are looking for, and they like what they hear when they call you, they'll drive miles and miles to come to you. It happened to me over and over.

## Who Are These Students?

They are people who come for a variety of reasons. I have tried to classify the reasons people seek tutoring and have come up with the following. They are students:

➢ who don't understand basic concepts

➢ who are full of anxieties

➢ in Learning Disabilities classes

➢ in Special Education classes

➢ who dropped out of high school and are studying for the GED (General Education Development test) which is equally acceptable as a high school diploma

➢ studying for the ACT and SAT tests

➢ who need help with their college courses

➢ who, as adults, are returning to school

➢ who are immigrants and need to learn English.

➢ who want to learn a craft, woodworking, computers, study the arts, and a myriad of other fields. Let's look at each category.

## Students Who Don't Understand Basic Concepts

It's hard to believe, isn't it, that there are people who don't understand the basic concepts of reading or math. As I've said before, they may be in junior or senior high school, but years earlier when they were supposedly learning to read or do math, they were just going through the motions. They didn't understand the lessons! Maybe they were too embarrassed to tell the teacher and somehow the teacher didn't pick up on their confusion. But that didn't matter. They were passed on to the next grade anyway. As each school year went by, they became more and more lost and bewildered until finally their parents or they themselves realized there was a real problem and called a tutor.

## Students Who Are Full of Anxieties

Book titles such as *How To Be Your Own Best Friend* proliferate to help people become happier and healthier, to have more friends and fewer problems. But where, oh where, are the books to help students who are so full of anxieties that they cannot concentrate on school work or tests or even relationships. These kinds of students have such problems! In school there may be a personality conflict with a teacher or classmate that affects their learning. Perhaps they feel that they are not living up to parental expectations. That alone can undermine their self-confidence. One of the main purposes of tutoring is to help these students rebuild their self-confidence so they can learn.

## Students in Learning Disabilities Classes

Can you picture the parents of students in these classes? Imagine having a child who cannot keep up with his schoolmates. Many of these parents may want outside help for their children. They want to give their children as many opportunities as possible to learn and succeed.

Did you know that some children in these classes have been carelessly put into classes in which they don't really belong? Instead of being "labeled," they need a teacher or tutor who really cares about them and gives them extra help. These kids aren't slow; they just need extra time to mature and learn.

## Special Education Students

Special Ed students really are special! And that's one of the biggest problems! They already know they're different. They are in special classes and special rooms. Their peers, the "normal ones," are far ahead of them in schoolwork and have friends of their own within their regular schoolrooms. These Special Ed kids are often called terrible names—"mentals"—"dummies!" Their egos are damaged. They try to hide it with glibness, but it shows through. You reach out to them, but at first they push you away. They're so afraid of rejection. They need a lot of love and patience before they'll believe how much you care.

They need to know you think they are important, that they are real people and fun to be with. And especially, they need to know that they can learn. It takes a little more effort to work with them, and it takes a lot more patience, but you get a bushel of rewards!

## High School Dropouts Who Are Now Studying for Their High School Diplomas

So many people drop out of high school! At the time, it seemed like the right thing to do. But later some of them want and need their diplomas. So they decide to study for the GED exams. These exams test English grammar, reading comprehension, vocabulary, geometry and algebra. This kind of tutoring can be especial fun. How many of the problems can you still do without a review? Test yourself as a tutor!

## Students Studying for the SAT and ACT Tests

Remember these tests? No matter how long ago you graduated from high school, you probably had to take them or ones like them. Talk about anxieties! After all, big rewards go with high scores. The college of one's choice! Or perhaps a scholarship! Juniors and seniors in high school may call on you because they want to get those high scores. Some may be retaking the test for an even better showing. They want the colleges to look very favorably upon them. And today, more than ever, it is getting harder to get into the college of one's choices; therefore getting as high a score as possible is very important.

## College Students

How many very young students do you think you can teach, one at a time, before you begin to wonder if you can still carry on some semblance of an adult conversation? So much of the time you are thinking on a child's level that you begin to wonder just how old you are! It's kind of scary, but in the funniest sense of the word! So when college-age students come along, ones with whom you can really converse in adult, grown-up terms, reach out! Embrace them with both arms! Don't just tutor them for the allotted time. Spend a few extra minutes just talking. Tutoring college students is a two-way street. They make you realize that you can still make it in the adult world; you are still a member of the well-informed, well-versed adult society.

Of course, the real reason college students are there is to learn. They're looking for someone who can help them in a particular subject, who can translate "psychologese" or "computerese" into a language they can understand, someone who will teach them the basics of English or math without demeaning them.

## Adult Students

I remember my grandmother, 70 years old, white hair in a bun, sitting in her rocking chair with my ten-year-old cousin next to her. Their heads were close together over a first-grade reader and as my grandmother put her finger on a very short word, my cousin would pronounce the word, one sound at a time.

My grandmother had come from Russia with her five very young, very lively children to join my grandfather who was already in this country. She raised her five children here. One became a doctor and another was one of the youngest teachers ever to have graduated from college in the state of Minnesota. The others worked so that their siblings could go to college. The working children married, had children of their own, and made sure that every one of them became college graduates too.

My grandmother always had the radio on and she was aware of the latest news, but she never had had the time to learn to read English. She treated all of her grandchildren — we numbered 14 — as though we were the greatest ever, and we had long conversations with her. But one of the sorrows of her life was that she couldn't read English. So, at 70, she was finally trying to reach that goal by sounding out one short word at a time with my 10-year-old cousin.

I tell you this true story because people of all ages have come to me to learn to read or write better. One elderly woman said, "I love to read, but I lose my train of thought by the time I come to the end of a page, and I find myself rereading all the time. It's taking me so long! Please, can you help me? I want to read faster and with more understanding, because there are so many good books and I want to read them all!"

Another woman in her late thirties wanted to improve her spelling. She was a file clerk and wanted to become a secretary. But her spelling was terrible. And she was tired of younger people getting the better jobs.

Men come for tutoring too. One man, who had a successful business, had never earned his high school diploma. And although very few people knew he hadn't graduated, he was aware of it. So every night for several weeks he came for tutoring. I cannot tell you how excited he was when he finally, at the age of 44, received his diploma.

## Immigrants Who Need to Learn English

The influx of people to our country is constant. They come mostly from Europe, the Orient, and Latin American countries. They come with some knowledge of English or with none. But they want to assimilate with our citizens and to communicate with them. They want jobs. They want friends. They need to be able to shop and to find their way around strange cities. When they find it necessary to travel, they want to be able to do so with the knowledge that they can be understood wherever they go.

Most immigrants go to night school several nights a week, but there are some who want more personalized instruction. They want to be free to ask as many questions as they want, to interrupt as often as they want, to learn at their own speed, and to be free to change the direction of the lessons if needed.

I have a Spanish-speaking student from South America who is having trouble with pronouns. I knew she was married, but I did not know who else lived with her. One day she said, " I have to get up at 5:30 in order to make her lunch." I asked who in her house had to leave for work so early. "My husband," she replied in her thick accent. She was chagrined when she realized that she had been using feminine pronouns to describe him. I'm sure she won't have that problem much longer!

Another of my students was an engineer who spoke several foreign languages. He had trouble with the English word "the" because it was not used in his native language. He said, "I go to store," or "I drive car to work." He, as do most newcomers to our country, had a hard time with idioms and slang expressions. Someone had asked him if he could "break a twenty." In his native tongue, that meant literally breaking the bill in pieces. Another time, I asked, "Did you understand the phrase we just used? Did you catch it?" He looked helplessly at his hands, knowing he had "caught" nothing.

Our language can be very difficult. Prepositions seem so simple, but just try explaining "at, in" or "on" to a foreigner. Does one come "in time," or "on time" and when does one know which word to use?

These students are eager. They want to learn, and so they make teaching a joy.

## People Who Want to Study New Fields

There is a myriad of people who want to learn something new that maybe they've wanted to do for a very long time or have just heard about. One day I was talking with a friend in an oil painting class I take, and she mentioned that she worked with miniatures. She showed me some of the wicker furniture she had just made for one of her tiny rooms. I became so intrigued that I decided to go to a class so that I could learn to work with miniatures too. Some people want to take up a sport for fun and fitness. There are so many things you can teach if you have the knowledge ... and patience.

As I've indicated, you can tutor in any subject with any person if you feel comfortable with the material and with the tutoring situation.

For example, I know very few words in Spanish. One day a student, whom I was seeing for reading and math, came to me, and said, "I'm failing Spanish. It really is foreign. Please, can you help me?"

I told her to bring her work along with her to the next session. She did. I looked at her Spanish book and discovered that — like English — Spanish verbs have different endings when used with different nouns and pronouns. The verbs and subjects have to agree also in number and in feminine and masculine forms. Therefore, to ask, "Es medico su padre?", which means "Is your father a doctor?", the word medico must be in masculine form and, of course, singular.

I quickly figured out the rules and then I was able to help my student. It really wasn't hard at all! Since then, I have helped others with their Spanish. Unfortunately, as quick as I was at learning to help my student, I didn't absorb it myself so I couldn't use it personally. Maybe next time!

If you want to make money doing something you enjoy, look at the field of tutoring. You have a world of choices, and people are out there waiting for you to let them know you're available.

## Chapter Eighteen

# Decisions: Where and When To Tutor; What to Charge

Anyone can take a classified ad in the paper, sit back and wait for the phone to ring. It seems so easy and quick! But before the phone rings, you must make all your decisions: where you are going to tutor, whom you will tutor, what you are going to charge, and what hours you will make yourself available.

## Where Are You Going To Teach?

There are several choices, but the two most common ones are either in your home or at your students' homes.

If you go to your students' homes, you may get more students because many parents and kids don't want to go elsewhere for tutoring. They may prefer seeing you in their homes because they don't want to lose time traveling. Let's face it, no matter what their ages, students would prefer to be with their friends as much as possible. So your coming to them is a time saver... for them.

BUT you may lose a lot of time going from one home to another when you could be teaching in your own office. In bad weather, the driving can be a hassle, and don't forget the cost of gas and oil and the wear and tear on your car.

Going to students' houses can cause a problem. Their friends may see you coming, know who you are, and what you do. You might become a source of embarrassment to the student. Students are also very easily *distracted* in their own homes. Friends come to the door, the telephone calls are for them, the family is walking around, and sometimes the cats and dogs plop down next to you and bark or purr, managing to disturb both you and your student. Their friends, playing outside and making happy noises, don't help either.

All in all, I prefer my own home. For the first year and a half, I taught in my recreation room, but my practice grew so large that I decided to move into an office building. I opened the doors in September when school started. For nine months I left for the office at 2:30 every afternoon and our son, Rob, who was then 12 years old, became a "latchkey kid." At 3:50 every day he called me to say he had arrived home safely from school. Two afternoons a week I rushed home at 4:30 to drive him to religious school, drop him off and then rush back to my office. My husband picked him up at 6:30. Every other day Rob either went to friends' homes or stayed home alone. Every evening my husband and son would come to my office building and we would eat dinner together. I stayed at the office until 10:00 Mondays through Thursdays and until 6:00 on Fridays and after four or five months, I began to hate the whole idea of working in an office. I hated the idea of Rob coming home to an empty house in the afternoons, and I hated not being home for dinner and the evenings with my husband and son.

One day when I had a few moments to myself, I sat down with paper and pencil and figured out that what I was paying in rent could be converted to payments on an addition to the house. My husband agreed. We hired a contractor and made our plans. The three of us were delighted when I moved my offices back home. Once again I worked in the recreation room waiting for the addition to be finished, but it didn't matter. I was home. We added a waiting room and office and a half-bath for my students. And in order not to disturb my family, we made an outside entrance directly into the waiting room.

When the students come to my home, they know they are there to work. There are few distractions. I have an

**173**

answering machine on my phone, so unless I am expecting a very important call, I turn the machine on while I teach. My family members know my schedule so they don't disturb me. If you decide to work out of your home, make sure you have a spot that is all your own. Whether it's a recreation room or any unused room, make sure it's an area where you will not be disturbed, and where it is quiet and pleasant, bright and cheerful. Atmosphere plays a big part in determining both your attitude and that of your students.

Do make sure your family and cats and dogs won't disturb you. We had a collie named Honey that the children grew to love. Many students would ask to pet her before we started to work. Then Honey would go out of the office. She knew her place! My students worried right along with us when Honey was sick, and they were as sad as we were when our dog finally died.

Another good reason for having students come to your home or office is that you can see more of them. If you have a place where students can wait, then you can teach one right after another. The younger ones may knock on your door a little too soon, but if you have books for them to color in or read or puzzles for them to do, they'll learn to wait patiently.

You may wonder what the parents do while waiting for their children. Well, fortunately, I now have a waiting room. But many of them do their grocery shopping or run other errands during the sessions. Before we built the addition, a few of the parents asked if they could wait in the living room. It was hard to say no, so I usually said yes, but it was hard on my husband and youngest son, Rob. Eventually we bought a small TV for Rob's room and put a small, very small, pool table in an unused bedroom. We didn't want our son to feel ignored just because I was teaching. And my husband was great! He would stay with Rob or read in the kitchen or bedroom, and sometimes he would go into the living room and talk to the waiting parents. The bonus was that we became very close friends with some of the parents. So weigh your options. Whichever one you choose must be the right one for you.

## Decide the Length of Your Sessions

Young children sometimes get very restless after 20 - 25 minutes. They will start asking what time it is and how much time they have left. Some students take five minutes or so just to get settled, no matter how old they are. And the much older students sometimes get so involved with what they are studying that you really want to give them as much time as possible. So I compromise at 45 minutes. With the very young ones, who have short attention spans, we often spend the last ten minutes playing some kind of learning game. Most of their learning is done in an enjoyable way anyway, but during this time, they can have *their* choice of any educational game. Fun and learning? They love it!

When I started my business, I also taught my older students for 45 minutes. They knew I would spend extra time with them if needed because I wouldn't stop teaching if we were in the middle of something important. After a few years, I discovered that my sessions with these students were always taking at least 50 to 55 minutes so I raised my fees and spent an hour with them. I still will go over the hour if I feel a student needs a few more minutes. Students also know that even if I fall behind during an earlier session, they will get their allotted time. When it's final time, report-card time, or time for the college entrance exams, I tend to lose time, so I make it up on my dinner hour. And the kids are terrific. They see me grabbing a quick sandwich and they'll tell me to take it easy, they'll wait.

## How Much Should You Charge?

This can be a tough question to answer when you first start tutoring, and there are several ways you can approach this.

You can call other individual tutors to find out what the going rate is. (You don't have to mention your name.) I'd like a dime for every person who has called me, said she was looking for a tutor, and then immediately asked, "How much do you charge?" or the people who have called, told me about their children's problem in about three sentences or less and then quickly asked my fees. It's fairly easy to tell that they are calling for information so that they themselves can begin tutoring.

I watch the classified columns closely and note that very soon after these calls there is a new ad for tutoring! I do appreciate those honest and forthright persons who say they are thinking about becoming tutors and wonder what the going rate is.

Some school teachers who also tutor charge less than private tutors because tutoring is just an "extra" job for them. Some teachers who are not currently working in a school system and perhaps are staying home to be with their own children, may want to teach only a few hours and so may also charge less. Private tutors who make this a full-time profession generally charge more.

There are other factors to consider too. Geography plays a big part in determining your fees. You may plan to tutor in a small town or a community where the average income is lower than in the major cities. You will have to adjust your fees accordingly. Regional differences exist as well. A small town in the South may differ from a small town in the Northeast.

When I began tutoring I charged $10 for 45 minute sessions; that enabled me to see some students more than once a week. My fees have increased over the years and I now charge $75 an hour.

You can also do your own market research. Ask parents what they would pay for help for their children. You can always raise the fees if you find that you are in demand or if you feel parents will pay you the extra money.

And there is a way to become in demand. Do something that is unique! Anyone can open a book and tutor. Anyone can advertise. But it is what *you* do that is *different* that will set you apart from the crowd! What do I do? I make myself available 7 days a week! That means if I see students on Monday and they run into problems on any other day, they can call me immediately. If I am teaching, I tell them I'll return their call between students or on my first break. If I am not home, they leave a message on my answering machine; they know they'll hear from me as soon as possible. We try to clear up the confusion by phone. We go over the material several times if necessary until the students understand the work. If they still don't understand, we set up an extra session.

If my students ask me to go to their schools to see them in plays or concerts, I try to go. If they ask me to call their teachers because they are afraid to ask them questions, I'll do that too. I do whatever I can to help.

I spend a lot of time on the phone with parents. If they are concerned about their child's schoolwork, or what is happening to their child socially, they may call for reassurance. I am not a counselor, but I have worked with so many types of students over the years that I can often spot trends and see behavior patterns. Parents appreciate my concern for their children, and I try very hard to develop good relationships with parents as well as with the children.

An important part of teaching is to let your students know that if they have a personal problem and need to talk about it, you will listen to what they have to say. My students know that I will never violate a confidence. Nothing they tell me goes further. Occasionally I may believe their problem is one their parents need to know about, so I'll suggest they talk to them. If they feel uncomfortable with this idea, I'll ask them if they want *me* to talk to their parents. As I said, I don't play psychologist, but I want the kids to know I'm on their team.

## Eileen Shapiro

When I began tutoring twenty five years ago, many people thought that $10 was too high and that I'd never get any students, let alone any twice a week! They were wrong! And in the ensuing years, I have become one of the highest paid tutors in my area.

You may hear many different reactions after you tell your callers your fees. Most callers will either accept them or tell you they cannot afford to spend that amount of money. A few get angry. "Are you kidding? What makes you think you or any other teacher is worth that kind of money?" And a very small number may ask if you will lower your fees. Some of these people really are having financial difficulties; the rest just want to pay less, "to get something for nothing." It's hard to judge which of these people is being totally honest in needing a reduced fee. You have to trust your intuition. But be careful. I once got caught badly.

It was September and school had just started when Mrs. Jennings called. She told me of her 11-year-old son's problems. Lou was in a fourth grade Special Ed class in what she referred to as an "uncaring" school.

His classmates made fun of him, his teachers weren't helping him, and the principal didn't want to get involved. Mrs. Jennings felt that Lou was standing still educationally and that he could read better and do more than the simple addition and subtraction problems he was being assigned. She believed that if Lou could see me twice a week, he would move forward more quickly. And then she seemed to grope for words. "We can't afford your fees. We have two older sons, and with my husband's salary, we just about make it." I listened attentively but said I wanted time to think about the fees. And then her voice became more anxious. "Oh, please," she implored, "Lou needs you so badly." And I fell for it—hook, line and sinker—and I lowered my fees.

Before Lou's first session, I called his teachers and went to his school to learn just what was happening in his class room. Then we began working together twice a week. Tutoring Lou was not easy. He was jumpy and irritable much of the time. Some sessions felt hours long.

And then it was Thanksgiving. We had an unexpected snowstorm; the winds were howling and the skies were gray. Mrs. Jennings came for Lou. She was wearing a full length mink coat. "Br-r-r!" she murmured. She pretended to shiver as she pulled her coat snugly around her. "I can't wait until Christmas vacation. We're taking our whole family to Mexico for two weeks!"

Can you imagine my reaction? Here I was, teaching Lou for much less than my ordinary fees, and his entire family was going to Mexico!

From that day on, when people ask me about lowering my fees, I respond by saying that when they come for the first session, we will discuss it. Those people who are in real need agree to that; those who are not never call again.

## Determine Your Schedule

Do you want to work only on weekdays? Do you want to work after school and/or in the evenings? Some tutors who have small children at home want to work when their husbands or wives are home to take care of the children. Others would rather work after school and hire sitters. Some do both. There are tutors who work on Saturdays and occasionally even on Sundays.

I decided to begin teaching as soon as school was over for the day, thinking I would be finished by dinner time. I soon discovered that many parents who work couldn't bring their children to me until evening. So I left my schedule flexible. At first my hours were scattered all over the clock, but within a year, my schedule was almost always filled from 3:30 til 10 p.m.

# Eileen Shapiro

While all of my children were still at home and in school, I didn't work on the weekends because I wanted that time with my family. When only my youngest was home and in high school, I began teaching SAT/ACT classes on Sundays. I did that because high school students are so involved during the week with homework, sports, and jobs that the only time most of them can come is on Sundays. A few years ago I added Saturday classes.

So when you make your schedule, keep all these points in mind. You may find yourself working hours you wanted to be free. Long, late hours can be tough. But when you look at your students, those hours can also be very rewarding.

## Chapter Nineteen

# Advertising: Making Your Debut

What do brochures, radio commercials, display ads, classified ads, Yellow Pages, community directories, and public relations activities have in common? They're all ways to advertise your services. They are ways to let the public know you are available. Let's take a look at these media.

## Brochures

You may be able to write some of a brochure yourself, but if you're shy about your accomplishments, ask someone who knows you to help with the writing. It's often hard to put on paper how good we are at what we do because it feels like we're being too egotistical. But it is important to tell people what your background is, what you have accomplished, and something about your philosophy, to—in short—sell yourself.

It is even more important to tell people the benefits that their children will receive from your tutoring. These benefits include increased self-confidence, better study habits, and learning how to study. Your tutoring gives students a firm basic understanding of their subjects. You can lessen students' test anxieties. And often, by coming to you, students can advance several reading or math levels in their classrooms. Benefits are extremely important. They are the reasons parents will choose you as their children's tutor.

One advantage of a brochure is its size. You can tell much more about yourself in a brochure than you can in a classified ad. Another advantage of the brochure is that you can use color. Choose your colors carefully because different amounts of a color can bring different reactions. It's important for you to know that artists and printers can use "percentages" of full colors for different effects. For example, if you want to use blue, 20 percent might be a light blue, 50 percent would be a medium blue, and 70 percent would be almost as bright a blue as possible. That way you can print three shades of blue on white paper; it will look like 4 colors, but you will be only paying for one.

Different color combinations bring different reactions, too. Blue and yellow together are bright and exciting; blue and green together are more subdued. Red often connotes danger, and orange can send out caution signals similar to road signs.

Paper comes in many colors too. You can use deep purple for your basic type with some printing in blue on a lavender paper and again it seems as though you are using three colors—which can be very expensive. However, all you've done is substitute lavender paper for white and used two colors of ink: deep purple and blue. Result: you have a three-color *effect* for just a two-color price.

Just as important as color is the headline you use on your brochure. In a newspaper the headline calls your attention to important events; in a brochure the headline grabs your attention to what is important about its contents. A poor headline would be, "Excellent Tutoring Available." It is too ordinary; it doesn't say much of anything. It certainly doesn't offer any solutions to the readers' problems.

I used "Your Child's Learning Problem Can Be Solved." That caught people's attention. Some people may have read my brochure and then discarded it. But many others were impressed. They said so when they called and started using my services.

# Advertising: Making Your Debut

When all the writing for your brochure is finished and you are ready to do the layout, find an artist to help you. After all, if your brochure is going to be on display for all to see, you want it to reflect a positive image of you. A printer can sometimes help you locate an artist. Or, see if you can hire an art teacher.

When your brochure is finished, talk to everyone you know —druggists, managers of retail stores and grocery stores, doctors and dentists — anyone who uses bulletin boards for displays or puts brochures on counters. Ask them if they will display your brochure. Walk around the shopping areas where your prospective students live and ask the local business people if they will display your brochures. Our doctor, a general practitioner, put my display holder on his waiting room counter. Another friend, the owner of a men's store, also put my brochures on display. So did our druggist. You can also do a direct mailing of brochures and even design one panel to use as your address space.

Remember, when you print a brochure, it's the initial cost that counts. Once you've spent the money to put it on the press, it's positively amazing how many more copies you can print for very little money. The additional cost for that extra 1,000 or 5,000 can be very small. Talk to your printer about this.

Write your brochure so it does not become outdated; then you can use it a long time without having to reprint. For example, don't quote fees. Put them on a separate sheet of paper. Don't print anything that can or will be changed.

In my first brochure, I wanted people to know that I had personal experience raising children, so I quoted my own kids' ages. A few years later, my two oldest children were married, and when I referred to them while discussing tutoring with parents, it showed how old the brochures were.

In my second brochure—which I used for my SAT/ACT classes — I mentioned eight three-hour sessions. When I reduced the number of sessions to seven, my brochures became outdated; once again, I had to throw out thousands of them.

So if you are very careful about what you write, you can print a few thousand brochures at a time. They will last for a long time and wind up being a big bargain.

## Newspaper Ads

When I first started tutoring, I did some market research and discovered that people seeking tutors usually looked in the want ads for this kind of service. Therefore, for many years a want ad was my one constant source of new students and the one form of advertising that I used consistently.

I ran my ad in a weekly newspaper that covered a group of different suburbs. When I first ran the ad, I placed it in several papers published by different companies. When someone called, I would ask that person where they had heard about me, and then I was able to determine which newspaper brought in the most business.

I had a discounted contract rate for my want ad because I ran it in the paper every week, all year 'round. My ad was so big that it always stayed at or near the top of the column called "Schools and Instruction," which is exactly where I wanted it. You can talk to the head of the classified ad department at your favorite paper to find out how to get your ad to the top of the school column in that paper.

It's utterly amazing what happens with an ad that you keep in the newspaper week after week. People phone you and say that they clipped out your ad months ago, put it away and then retrieved it when they decided to call you. Many others will say that they had seen the ad many times and then thought of it when they actually needed help.

You see, just the fact that the ad is there every week means that people know you're established and reliable.

# Advertising: Making Your Debut

Three or four weeks may pass by without a phone call, and then suddenly the phone can ring constantly.

Place your ad when *you* feel you are ready to begin tutoring. I placed my first ad so that it ran the last week of May. Most of my friends thought that was a foolish time to advertise. School was out, students were going away to camp or on vacation, and everyone wanted a break from studies. I wish I had a dollar for everyone who said to wait until September or who said I was throwing money away because I was advertising too soon.

I, however, had been researching for three months. I had talked to elementary and secondary school counselors and to officials of tutoring centers. There were a few counselors who told me that my idea of charging $10 for 45 minutes was unreasonable. (Remember, this was in the early '70s.) If people wouldn't pay that much for one session, how could I possibly expect to see students two or more times a week if they needed that much help? And have students come to my house? Forget it! The more I researched, the more negative comments I got. And who needed that? So I took the proverbial "bull by the horns" and ran my ad.

I mentioned having a catchy headline for your brochure. The same thing applies to your want ad. Most of the people who run ads use headings like "Tutor," "Reading Specialist," "Special Education Teacher," etc. Readers see a lot of similar ads, but if you write something that really has appeal, you will get many calls. I used the same headline as in my brochure and my want ad: "Your Child's Learning Problem Can Be Solved."

I changed my headline only once. I decided to try a different approach. An interesting thing happened. I didn't get any calls! When I realized that this was peak season and my phone was too quiet, I knew I had made a mistake. I changed the headline back to the "old reliable" and the calls began again. I asked some of the callers where they had seen the ad and what they liked about it. I discovered that some of them had seen the ad some time before, and when they looked for it again, the ad was not running. They didn't see the headline that had caught their eye. So, luckily for me, they waited a while, and when they saw the original ad, they called.

What I am saying is so very simple. When you find a good, eye-catching headline, stick with it.

As good as your headline may be, you still need good copy to follow it. You should state your qualifications and what you have decided to teach. Even if you are an English teacher, you can teach history, social sciences, and any other subject that requires reading. After all, if a child is having trouble in these classes, it may be that he simply cannot comprehend what he is reading. And if you are a math teacher, you can teach science, physics, and chemistry, too. Aren't all formulas based on math? And aren't all theories and story problems really exercises in training students to read carefully and with under-standing? *Don't be afraid to diversify.*

You may want to print your name along with your phone number in your ad. I never used my name. I believe there are disadvantages to having your name and number together. I always introduce myself on the phone and I always ask the name of the caller. That seems a little more personal to me.

Give free rein to your imagination when you begin to write your ad. Put in everything you'd say if you had all the space you wanted. Then start editing it down. What is absolutely essential? What makes your ad stand out? Have you written everything the reader needs to know? Will the reader understand abbreviations? Don't use them if you can avoid them. Above all, is your ad strong enough to pull in clients?

Once you have placed the ad in the paper, give it time to work. Don't rush to change anything unless you can see that it desperately needs revision. After several weeks, if nothing happens, think about making changes, subtle ones that will make the ad more effective. In time, you will perfect your ad.

Incidentally, I checked my ad every week. I wanted to see that the printer hadn't made an error and that the ad was inked properly so that it was legible. Every so often, I noticed that someone was using part of my ad in their own copy. At first, I was very irritated. Then I realized that imitation is the sincerest form of flattery. My ad must have been great! Now whenever I see something lifted from any advertising I do, I think to myself, "Another one with no mind of her own!"

## Direct Mail

Direct mail is a wonderful, fast and inexpensive way to get to your targeted audience. When I decided to teach classes for the college entrance exams, I wanted to attract all the juniors in our suburb and surrounding ones who would be taking the SAT/ACT exams. Because it was the first time I had ever run classes, because I only had ten days in which to advertise and because I was new at this game, I thought a display ad in the local newspaper would do the trick for me. So I decided to run that kind of ad on two consecutive Thursdays. The salesman for the local weekly chain of newspapers claimed that if I made the ad large enough (one eighth of a page, 4 x 5 inches) and ran it in all the nearby suburbs, many of the readers would see it. The papers in those areas were delivered to approximately 120,000 households, so I'd get great coverage. What he didn't mention was that in many of those households there might not be students interested in these tests and also that it was very easy to miss an ad altogether unless people read every page.

Nevertheless, I tried this way of advertising twice. The first time was in the spring when most students take the tests. I had six students. The second time, in the fall of that year, I had 21 students. Then I learned that direct mail was less expensive and much more effective. I could directly reach the students' homes rather than use a display ad that many readers could overlook.

So how does one use direct mail? First define your audience. It can be all the elementary students in nearby schools; it can be all the high school students; or it can be a specialized group of students. Once you know whom you want to attract, contact a direct mail house that sells lists of names. Tell them what you need — which groups, what zip code areas, and how many students or parents you want to inform about what you do.

Now, decide how you want to inform your audience. You can inform them with your brochure or you can send them a letter, or you can do both. Whichever you decide to use, don't do any writing yourself, unless you are an excellent copywriter. Too many people try to save money by doing all the writing themselves and then they fail. Even though I do a lot of writing and have been published several times, I hire a copywriter, one who is an expert in direct mail. He knows what people will read and he knows how to get their attention. My copywriter has used several different copy approaches for my business.

When I first decided to use direct mail, I sent parents a letter enclosing a prepaid and pre-addressed postcard that could be returned to me. The letter stated that the parents could either call me for more information, or they could return the postcard with their name and address, and I would send the information to them.

For a few years, I didn't mind the tremendous amount of work this two-process direct mail entailed. But the phone calls added a lot of time too, and I decided to see if I could cut down on the amount of time I was using answering mail and calls. We stopped sending letters and began using an eight by fourteen-inch brochure folded down to five by eight inches. It listed all my credentials, how I conducted classes and recommendations from both parents and students. The registration form was printed right in the brochure and, once people decided to use my services, they had the forms right at their fingertips. I sent out these brochures twice, once to inform the public of what I did and again to remind them of my classes. I later found that sending a reminder *postcard* instead of a printed brochure for the second mailing worked — sometimes even better. And it saved a lot of money.

You'll also need to find a reliable mailing service that will pick up your material, do all the labeling, affix postage, and transport your mail to the post-office. Sometimes these mailing services will help you choose the most accurate and complete mailing lists you want and can order them for you directly. Like anything else, research these services and get lots of references. You want someone who is reliable and preferably has been in business for a long time. This mailing is *important* to you and *costly*, so make sure you get the best.

## Radio or Television Commercials

Another way of advertising is using radio or television commercials. I have never tried television commercials because they are very expensive; direct mail is much more effective for less money.

I once tried a spot announcement on FM radio. I used a classical music station that has a wealthy, highly-educated audience known for its loyalty to the advertisers using the station. As a matter of fact, the radio station itself asked me for letters of recommendation before it would play my commercial. The salesman said I would find that if the listeners liked my commercial and called to inquire about my services, I could bet money they would come from almost any distance.

Sure enough, he was right. One person who called came for an interview with her son. She then brought him to me twice a week, driving 27 miles each way for almost a year.

By the time he was ready to stop seeing me, his fees alone had more than paid for the commercial.

The cost of a radio commercial will vary, of course, depending on many factors: the station you are using, the time of day and the number of times a day your commercial is aired, and so on. Even the time of year changes the costs which can be quite high.

If you are going to use radio ads, you need to have your commercial aired often enough so that people really notice it. Running it once or twice is not the answer. Constant repetition is what is needed.

## Public Relations

Most people think of publicity as advertising. Yes, some advertising is used only as a way to enhance your image. Some methods include leaflets, brochures, and feature stories in newspapers.

A "news-peg" is a good way to get information about you and your service into the newspapers. A "news-peg" is a statement that you can make about education and then work in your own story. For example: "Students are getting better grades in school this year than they did last year. However, they are having a harder time getting into the colleges of their choice." Then you can talk about what *you* are finding out from the students that you teach.

A second way of getting into the papers is to contact the reporter on education. When you call, these are the things to ask:

1.   Have you reached the correct person? If not, who is that person?
2.   Does the reporter have the time to talk? Reporters work on ridiculous deadlines, so they will tell you when they can talk to you.
3.   When the reporter does have time, would he or she be interested in listening to an idea you have, and then, if it's appealing, would it be okay to

write a short article about it and then turn the
story in?

**4.** If the reporter does not like the idea, can he
suggest a better one?

Another way to become known is by being interviewed
on television. The program director or host/hostess is your
contact. These interviews require a lot of preparation. You
are not simply being quoted in an article; you are being
heard by every listener. The very moment you say
something, it goes out over the airwaves. And if you're on
television, every expression on your face is seen by the
viewers. Your words and expressions help create your
image. So, before you are interviewed, try to find out as
much as you can about the questions that you will be
asked. Compose your answers and then ask someone to
role-play with you. If possible, do this on a cassette
recorder or video tape recorder. Rehearse as often as you
can. It will help you feel confident when you are in the real
situation.

Your goal is always to become so articulate and
knowledgeable that editors and reporters *call you
directly* to ask for interviews. I, along with other
educators, was invited to a meeting with media represent-
atives from many radio and television stations in Chicago.
We spoke about our views on education and students and
schools. It was fun, it was interesting, and it was
informative.

A few weeks later, I was called by a local television
personality who has her own public affairs interview show.
She asked me to be on her program. However, she did not
give me a list of the questions she was going to ask, only an
overview of the topics. I sure was nervous! But I knew my
subject well and was confident in what I believed. With no
rehearsal whatsoever, my interview, according to my
hostess, was great! I did so well that I got calls from parents

who had seen the show and later brought their children to me for tutoring. The moral is that if you become well known, reporters and editors will come to you.

A fourth way to get recognition is to give speeches. You can contact the program chairpersons of organizations such as the PTA, women's clubs, the Rotary, the Lions, charity groups, and others. Figure out what these audiences want to hear and write your speech before you contact the program chairman to see if she'll book you. Make your speech no longer then 20 minutes, plus a question and answer period. People lose interest quickly if your speech is too long. And remember to bring your brochures. This is a golden opportunity to hand them out! Be sure to send notices about your speeches to the newspapers. This will further enhance your image as an expert.

So what is public relations? Interpreting your business to its public(s) and interpreting the public(s) back to you and your business.

## Miscellaneous Advertising

There are some other forms of advertising you should know about before moving on. They are:

> ➤ Yellow Pages ads and listings,
> ➤ Ads or listings in community directories,
> ➤ High-school newspapers, and
> ➤ Church or synagogue bulletins.

## Yellow Pages

These listings or ads may be valuable to you and are certainly worth checking into. Be sure you find out from callers, however, whether the Yellow Pages were responsible for their calls. I tested these listings and I was unable to rely very much on them for getting new students. I got one in all the years I used it. However, something happened that was even more exciting than getting new students. What happened as a direct result of that ad was the beginning of a new direction for me in tutoring, and what several years later, is almost the total thrust of my business.

That day when I answered the phone, the voice on the other end said, "I saw your ad in the Yellow Pages of the local phone directory. I'm a high school math teacher, and I wondered if you hire teachers for tutoring."

What was uncanny about this was that I had just been thinking of tutoring for the SAT/ACT tests and hiring someone to help me so that I could teach small groups of students. I had given this a lot of thought and knew that *I* could teach both the math and verbal portions of the test. I also knew that if I hired someone to work with me, I could make more money by having more students at one time. And here was a teacher calling out of the blue!

She said that she had a baby at home, so she only wanted to teach a few hours a week. She also mentioned that nights and weekends were great because then her husband would be at home with their child. I asked her to come for an interview.

Everything worked out well and, because I wanted to announce my classes immediately, I put a display ad in the local paper. Two weeks later, my classes began. They were small the first time because I relied on only a display ad, but my classes have grown considerably since then.

That is the only other time the Yellow Pages worked for me in the many years that I have been tutoring. But what a way for it to work! I am now known as a college entrance exam specialist, teaching approximately 25 individual students a week and two to four classes of 16 students several times a year.

## Community Directories

Don't overlook your community directories. Quite often a city, village, or civic group will publish a catch-all directory of local merchants, churches, doctors, drug stores, etc. Find out if such a directory exists by calling your own city hall officials and/or local chamber of commerce.

## High School Newspapers

Almost every high school publishes a newspaper and to pay the publishing costs, the students sell advertising space. This is a terrific way to get directly to the students. They all read the paper to find out what is happening in their school, when and where. Most likely they will see your ad. The problem is that the kids don't always take the paper home or communicate to their parents that there is a tutor advertising in the paper. When students need a tutor, they or their parents usually ask other students and parents for the names of tutors they are using. However, this is still a good avenue to investigate; just because it doesn't work for all tutors doesn't mean it won't work for you.

## Church and Synagogue Bulletins

Last, but not least, are the publications sent out by churches and synagogues. Many of these bulletins underwrite their costs by advertising. Of course, the price of advertising varies so, if possible, check the number of readers who have children to see if it pays to place your ad there. These publications go into many homes and are read by many people, some of whom may just happen to be looking for a tutor for their children, for either religious or academic classes.

## Word of Mouth

The best kind of advertising, naturally, is the kind that is free. And that occurs when one of your students tells another student about you, or when one parent tells another. Can you imagine how good it feels when I get a call from someone who says, "Mrs. Jones told me how great you're doing with her child. I have a child who needs help too." Or when a student of mine says, "I have this friend who knows I see a tutor. She asked me about you, and I told her you can teach anything! Her name is Annie Burns, and she is going to call you. I hope that's okay." Okay? I love it. The problem is that if you're not careful, you can get overloaded.

A year ago, a woman from a suburb quite a distance away called and said she got my name from her friend who lived near me. Her son needed help with his ACT test and she asked if I could help him. I had not taught any students from her area because of its distance, nor had I sent any direct mail to the homes in that school district. But I decided that if she didn't mind her son driving all the way to my office, why shouldn't I teach him? And so we began. Two weeks later, Jason's best friend, Guy, called. He, too, wanted help. A month later the boys took the test and a month after that, they both called excitedly. They had done so well that they knew they would be able to go to the schools they desired. Their parents were delighted—and so was I.

That was in late spring. Fall came. In November, my phone started to ring and didn't stop. Jason's mother had spread the word about me, and within two weeks, I had 15 students just from Jason's school. I already had ten students from other schools and in addition to this, I was getting ready to teach classes. I had a very full schedule, and yet I kept trying to squeeze kids in everywhere. When more parents called, I told them I was really sorry but I didn't have any more free time. It seemed incredible to me, but many of them insisted on waiting for me, so I began to put names on a waiting list.

This sounds great. It was—for about 4 months. I was working from 9:00 to 4:00 on Sunday and from 2:00 to 9:00 p.m. Mondays through Fridays.

And then one day I looked at my husband and said I felt like I was going to collapse. I loved what I was doing, I loved the kids, but I sure didn't love me. Luckily, I have a great husband. He sent me on a vacation for a week. He said my students would not suffer if I was gone for a week. In fact, they would gain from my being fresher. Of course, he was right! So learn to pace yourself and know your limits.

Word of mouth *is* great. It shows that people think highly of you and that you are doing a good job.

Chapter Twenty

# Dealing with the Public

"HELP! The phone's ringing! What'll I say?"

Your ad is running, and your brochures are out! Everyone can see there's a new tutor in town! Does that mean the phone will ring off the hook? Maybe.

My ad appeared on Thursday morning. I clutched the paper. I scanned all the want ads. There it was. My ad —big, bold, and brassy. Too brassy? No. I thought it looked confident. But would others feel the same way? How long before the phone would ring? Doubts invaded.

I needed one and a half sessions a week just to pay for my ad. I didn't even think about the cost of the brochures! I told myself, "It's done. Don't keep staring at the phone." But to no avail. I tried to console myself with the excuse that the ad was brand new and it might take time for people to notice it. By 6 o'clock that evening, I had lowered my sights. I'd be satisfied if someone would just call for information. By 9 o'clock I had given up hope that there would be any response. I was dejected. I wanted this venture to flourish, and I wanted it to happen right away!

At 9:30 the phone rang! The call was for tutoring! I'd read about a "pounding heart" and a "racing pulse," and now it was happening to me. I braced myself, made sure my voice would sound calm and confident. Five minutes later, I had my first student — a second grader who needed help in math. I was ecstatic! I was on my way.

The next day, I didn't watch the phone. After all, I had one new student. I didn't want to push my luck, and besides, how many did I need to make a start? At noon the phone rang. Moments later I had my second student — a seventh grader who needed help badly with study habits

**197**

and skills. Two months later, at the end of July, I had four students, a total of eight sessions per week. Who said it couldn't be done?

Since the beginning of my practice, I have found that the way I talk to people on the phone is very important. A phone can be so impersonal. Callers have no idea to whom they're speaking; they can't see you, they only hear your voice. And with your voice alone, you have to sell yourself. Make sure you sound very interested, very confident, and very knowledgeable.

Over the years, I have talked to numerous callers. And I have found that there are many types. After a while you can almost classify them. There are callers who want quick answers for problems that have been going on for years. There are those who only want basic information: your fees, length of sessions, your home or theirs. There are callers who want to pick your brain and start their own tutoring practices. Some people call who simply want someone to listen while they pour out their problems. They'll discuss all the difficulties they and the schools are having with their children or the difficulties their children themselves are having. When they finally hang up, they'll feel better having dumped on you. You will likely have one of these reactions: (1) good feelings, because you have helped and maybe you'll get a new student; (2) exhaustion, because listening can be very tiring; (3) disgust, because you've been on the phone so long and you didn't get a new student.

Let me give you an example. When I first started tutoring and my practice was growing quickly, I listened to everyone. I felt every call was a potential student. How soon I learned! I was a free therapist! One woman called me every five or six months for about two years. Every conversation was the same and always ended on the same note. "I am going to wait one more week. If things don't change, I am going to see the teachers and then I will bring my daughter to you." I came to dread hearing her voice on the phone, yet I never kept the conversations short. Incidentally I never did meet her daughter.

Another parent whose son I was teaching would call at least once a week to talk about the difficulties her family was having. I spent a good 25 minutes on the phone with her every time she called. This went on for quite a while before I realized what was happening. Instead of seeing a counselor, she was telling her woes to me. And I was getting involved in something that was not in my field. That's when I finally put an end to calls that were not directly related to my teaching. I also put a time limit on all my calls. Five to ten minutes is now the maximum time I stay on the phone.

Let me suggest this: If people want to use your services, they will say so in five to ten minutes. If they still want more information, ask them to come in for a consultation. If they really want help, they'll come. If not, at least you haven't lost much time.

Now don't be surprised if, when you first take calls about tutoring, you are a little hesitant with some of your answers. It takes a little time to recognize the different types of callers. Little by little you will develop your own way of conversing with them, and you'll also polish your replies so that every caller hears how positive you feel and how knowledgeable and concerned you are about each student.

Incidentally, if you are really nervous about these first calls, a good way to minimize that is to role play with a family member or friend. Ask him or her to play "devil's advocate" and ask you questions that take much thought to answer. After you have had time to think through your answers, you will be more at ease when a "true" caller phones you about tutoring.

When people actually do call you about tutoring, they usually have many questions. The first two almost always are about your fees and scheduling. After those the most often-asked questions are these:

**1. "Do you work with students who are in Special Education or Learning Disabilities classes?"**

If you have never worked with these students and don't want to, say so. But if you do teach them, be sure to say up front whether you have a degree in those fields. You **do not need** such a degree to be successful. If you have worked with these young people before, tell the caller about your experiences. It's a good time to give him/her an overview of any special philosophy or talents you have. The callers must be reassured that you know what you are doing and are confident that you can help. (If you would like to work with these students and do not have a degree in Special Education or Learning Disabilities, refer to Chapter Six.)

**2. "Do you work with children of all ages?"**

That answer depends strictly on what you like to teach and to whom. Again, you must be comfortable with your choice.

**3. "If the student can't read or understand what he is reading, can you make a diagnosis of the problem over the phone?"**

If you think you can make a tentative diagnosis over the phone, such as, "It sounds as if the student is having trouble with comprehension or making inferences," remember to emphasize that your diagnosis is tentative and that you will know more after you have seen the student and worked with him. I'm going to repeat this: Make sure your caller understands that your diagnosis is tentative; you do not want parents to say later that you positively diagnosed a problem that you merely had said was a possible problem.

**4. "How long do you think it will take my child to catch up with his class?"**

It's not a good idea to commit yourself. Some students learn faster than others, some are more committed than others, and some need to build their confidence before they really start learning. Don't even try to estimate a time. What if you were to say three months, twice a week, and it took the student six months to catch up? Even after I have worked with a student for a few weeks, I don't give "graduation" dates. As soon as I see growth in learning and self-confidence, I tell the parents. But most of the time, I don't even have to do that. The students and the parents themselves see the changes and tell me!

## 5. "How many times a week do you see a child?"

To answer this, you need to consider the student's age, grade level, and the seriousness of the problem. If you feel the student cannot retain material from one week to the next, then seeing him twice a week is important. You can qualify that by saying that when the child shows he is learning and making progress consistently, you will be able to cut the number of sessions. There are some parents who think their child is in such dire straights that they themselves set up a schedule of two to three times a week on their first call. They believe the extra help is that necessary.

Sometimes parents or students themselves tell you that, no matter how difficult the problem is, they can only afford one session per week. If you want to teach these students, you must respect those terms. It's surprising how much learning a student can accomplish once a week if he is properly motivated.

## 6. "Do you write contracts for a certain number of sessions?"

I never use contracts for individual sessions. Contracting for a certain number of sessions can pose a problem. What if you contract to teach students for 10 sessions and find that they only need 6 or 7 sessions to correct their problems? Or what if you say, for example, that you can teach fractions in 5 lessons and find you have a slow student who needs 7 or 8 or even 9 lessons? Contracts can hurt your credibility. I have found that it's safer to say that you'll know more after you see a student, and even then, you can't really say for sure. You will keep in close contact with the parents so they'll always know how their children are progressing.

I have told every parent whose child I have taught that I don't believe in keeping students any longer than necessary. My goal is and has always been to teach students so well that they can do their schoolwork without my help. Of course, they also know I'm immediately available if a problem recurs.

### 7. "Do you test the student? If not, do you need test scores from school? Do you need or want papers or report cards?"

Do you want to test students? I don't. I believe the students are so anxious when they first come to me that testing them only adds to their anxieties. Testing is not always accurate anyway, and after I have seen the student, talked with him and watched him work, I can diagnose what the problem is.

Do you want test scores from the school? Sometimes these test scores are helpful. I use them to see how well a student takes tests. Is he consistent in his test-taking? Is he good in one subject and better or worse in others? Is there a wide disparity in scores? The one thing I do not do is use the scores to determine my students' capabilities. Until I have worked with them for a while, I really don't know if they become anxious when they take tests or if they really don't know the material because of lack of study skills. I try to figure out the answers to these questions by myself.

Do you need papers or report cards? I use papers only to see what kids are being taught in school and *how*. It helps to know what is going on in the classroom. Report cards are sometimes not objective enough, so if you decide you want them, be sure to look at them only as one possible measure of a child's abilities.

### 8. "How do you teach a child self-confidence?"

Self-confidence, I tell callers, comes with learning. As the students begin to understand their work and are able to participate in class more freely, they become more self-confident. It may take time, but I tell parents that once the self-confidence begins, the learning progresses more quickly. Learning and self-confidence go hand-in-hand and soon the self-confidence spills over into *all other areas* of the students' lives.

☆  ☆  ☆

Mary Beth, whose father was a friend of my husband, was in one of my SAT/ACT classes. She was a pretty but quiet girl who attended a parochial school. Because she lived quite a distance away, she didn't know any of the other students in her class. When the class started, Mary Beth spoke with the other students only when she needed to but as the hours passed by she became more friendly and outgoing. One of the boys in the class was attracted to her and she appeared to like him, too. But his manners left something to be desired. He was loud and rude. Even though this bothered Mary Beth somewhat, when he asked her to meet him at the local hamburger stand, she agreed. I was disturbed because they had met in my class, and I didn't want that to be the cause of a problem.

Mary Beth and Ned began to go on dates together and continued to do so even after the classes ended. For a few weeks I wondered about these two, but I didn't feel like there was anything I could do.

And then one day, Mary Beth's father called. He wanted to thank me for all the help I had given his daughter. "Mary Beth's scores on the exams went up considerably and so did her grades in school. And has she ever gotten a lot of self-confidence since being in your classes." When I asked what he meant, he replied, "You know that Mary Beth has been going out with a boy from your classes. Well, one night they went out and Ned was extremely loud and obnoxious.

In the past, Mary Beth would have accepted that but **not this time!** She called home and asked me to come and pick her up. I was really proud of her. She speaks up for herself now, she knows what she wants, and she feels great about herself. And it's all because of you! Thanks again."

What I said is true. Learning and self-confidence do go hand-in-hand.

### 9. "The SAT/ACT exams are three to four months away. How many individual sessions will a student need?" or "How many weeks are your classes?"

In Chicago the number of sessions depended on the students. Most of them had taken the PSAT and/or PACT and had some idea of the scope of their problems and where they needed to improve their scores. Many of them —high scorers and low—would start four to five months ahead of the SATs and ACTs and then come every week.

In Los Angeles, many parents only wanted their children to come four to six times. I found that amount of time was just not enough. The kids would be just beginning to catch on to the concepts of the tests and then would have to quit. I told parents that so few sessions would just be throwing their money away. So I decided to make teaching these tests a set of 10 sessions. Unless parents are willing to meet that contract, I will not teach their children. Now and then some students do come for a few extra meetings, but 10 sessions usually is enough. If students are only studying for a part of the tests, we make special arrangements.

The individual sessions can be costly for some parents so they may prefer classes. My classes now run for 18 hours: three hours once a week for six weeks. The cost of the 18 hours of classes (and sharing that time with seven other students) is the equivalent of about seven individual sessions.

# Dealing with the Public

Since I moved to Los Angeles, I schedule four classes: two on Saturdays and two on Sundays—one in the morning and one in the afternoon with a maximum of 16 students in a class. Eight are in math and eight are in English for one and one half hours and then they switch classes. Because the classes fill quickly, I cannot always give the people who call a choice of classes. Those who call too late must decide what they can afford and what they want to do. Some sign up for individual tutoring and some wait for the next test.

## 10. "Will you be in contact with the teachers?"

Callers have different views on this question. Some want you to communicate as quickly as possible with the teachers to learn how their children are doing in school and to try to get further insight into their difficulties. There are always a few parents or students who believe they don't know the right questions to ask a teacher so they want you to be the contact. And there are some who think they do not clearly understand what the teacher is trying to say. They feel that you, as their child's tutor, would be able to talk one-on-one with the teacher and clarify any difficulties the child is having.

On the other hand, there are parents who want you to stay away from the schools. Some are very upset with the school system and they want a tutor who will help their child without getting the school involved. Others simply believe that it's not the school's business to know what they do after hours with their children. In a large city where there are many schools, you can choose to remain anonymous and uninvolved with school personnel. However, in a small community, where "everyone knows everyone," this is more difficult.

I do not use the schools for referrals; therefore I can be a child advocate. I can go to schools and when discussing my students I can be on their side. Because I see these youngsters from a different angle than the school personnel do, I can present a different view.

Eileen Shapiro

School administrations themselves have different views about tutoring. Some welcome you with open arms. Others want no part of outside tutors. And yet parents have every right to seek this help. Therefore, it is important that you know as much as possible about the school system. You could find yourself in a situation like this:

☆  ☆  ☆

Cheryl Greene came to me when she had been in the second grade for about two months. She was in a learning disabilities class an hour a day. Her mother told me that Cheryl's self-confidence was nil. Her teacher had even had the gall to tell Cheryl *she would never be able to go to college.* Luckily for Cheryl, her parents felt she could learn and grow and they sought outside help.

According to Mrs. Greene, the school could not know that I was working with Cheryl. If school authorities learned that she was receiving help after school, she would be taken out of the learning disabilities class and would get no extra help in school. The rule at that school was that if any child had a tutor after school hours, the time allotted for helping that child in school should go to someone who was not getting help elsewhere.

Mrs. Greene and I had to tell Cheryl to be very secretive about her tutoring. Cheryl really liked her learning disabilities teacher and didn't want to give her up. So, we worked together for the entire year in a veil of secrecy. And then it was June. Cheryl's teacher called Mrs. Greene, telling her she believed that Cheryl should have a tutor for the summer. Because Cheryl had suddenly been doing better, the teacher didn't want the momentum to stop. She even suggested names of tutors.

Mrs. Greene then told her that since Cheryl had been to see me, she wanted her to continue to work with me. "Fine. That's good," the teacher replied. "If you will have Mrs. Shapiro call me, I'll be glad to fill her in and explain what we are doing here in school." So finally, eight months after I had started working with Cheryl, I was able to contact the teacher.

☆ ☆ ☆

So you see, in order to help your students, it is important to know the policies and politics of the different school systems.

In summary, be prepared with the answers to the questions parents ask. If you *are* prepared, you will be the kind of tutor parents want.

## Chapter Twenty-One

# Volumes and Volumes: Books and Materials

A small shelf held all of my books when I began tutoring. I owned two readers, a few math books, a dictionary and a set of encyclopedias. In the ensuing years, my tutoring library has enlarged to take up almost two full walls; each section is eight feet wide by six feet high. Everyone who comes into my office is amazed at the wealth of material there.

Included on the shelves are books for almost every conceivable subject. There are books on physics, chemistry, algebra, statistics, complete sets of books for teaching reading and math, foreign language books, grammar texts and literature books. There are dictionaries and a thesaurus for every reading level from pre-readers to college level students. There are workbooks for every level student in most subjects too. There are remedial books everywhere. And besides books, I have all the materials the student might need. For example, I have compasses, rulers, colored pencils and pens, crayons, colored index cards, and all sorts of paper—graph, lined, unlined, colored and poster board. In short, I have enough material to open my own school!

"But the expense?" you think. Ah, but it's not as expensive as you imagine.

"And the sources! Wherever did you go to get all your resources?" Would you believe me if I told you that finding the books was never a problem. The problem was where to put them all!

# Volumes and Volumes: Books and Materials

So where and how do you get your supplies?

## Schools

One of the first places I went for books was the school itself. After a student showed me the book he was using, I would call his principal and ask if I could borrow the books my student was using. Often a principal would gladly lend them to me if there were any extra copies. The only thing he or she would ask is that I return them at the end of the school year.

Over the years in Chicago, I had become good friends with the principal of the nearby school, the one in which my own children were students. The principal knew I was tutoring and when I asked for a book, he would not only lend me that one, but would also give me other books that were no longer being used. In that way, I was able to get a full set of reading and math books for elementary students. He also gave me extra, unused handwriting books and old unused workbooks.

My students themselves gave me their books at the end of the school year instead of selling them, and of course, I accumulated my own children's schoolbooks.

## Stores that Sell Publishers' Overstocks

Another great source for books is the stores that carry publishers' overstocks and books that schools no longer want. This type of store may exist only in larger cities, so call the manager of your local bookstore and see if his store or some others carry these types of books or can obtain catalogs for you. I've gone into these stores just to browse and often found myself carrying shopping bags full of books when I left. Often I found a book that had only one section that looked particularly useful, but I would buy it anyway. I thought it might come in handy sometime. These stores sometimes even carry books in use at the current time. I paid about 20 percent of the publisher's actual price for the books, so you'll know why I frequented these stores.

## Publishers of Textbooks

Write or call the publishers of textbooks and ask them to send you their most recent catalogs. There may be times when you will need a particular book which is only available directly from the publisher. It is a good idea to phone the publisher the first time because you can then ask for the name of the general sales manager and ask to be connected to that person. Introduce yourself, telling him that you are a legitimate tutor with only the highest of ethics. The sales manager may ask you to send proof of who you are and what you do. Stationery with your logo or title will often be enough. The reason for doing this is so that you will have a contact person at each publisher who will recognize your name and have the authority to sell you books when you make a request.

It won't be easy to obtain teachers' editions. Some publishers will send them only to school personnel. Publishers do not want to get caught in the trap of selling teachers' editions to just anyone. Teachers' editions contain answers, and what if the purchaser is just a student who wants answers! But if the manager knows you, he will send you teachers' editions. The cost of books through a publisher is often the same to you as to the schools: 25 percent off the retail cost.

Watch closely to see which publishers the schools are using. There are many publishers that are not quite as well known as others but have a great selection of books for special needs. At one time, I was teaching a boy who had been in a car accident and was homebound. When I went to his school to pick up his books, I found that his reading was at third grade level, but only his science teacher was using a book that he could read easily. The content of the book followed closely the curriculum of the regular eighth grade, but was written at his level of reading. I noted the publisher's name, wrote for a catalog in which I found lists of books on geography, history and health written in the same manner as the science book, eighth grade curriculum but 3rd grade reading ability. I now keep this catalog with all my others. Incidentally, every year publishers add new books and stop publishing others; therefore it pays to ask for new catalogs.

## Any Store that Sells Books

Department stores, drug stores, discount stores, (e.g., K-Mart, Woolco, Walmart) sell books. They carry the kind that parents like to buy for their children to use as practice books. Or they may have the small "easy to read" books. I have gone to these stores and picked up these books for a quarter to fifty cents. Sometimes these inexpensive books are on sale. For example, books that are a quarter may be on special, three for a quarter. You can buy several and ask the younger children to read them to you. When they finish reading and you've discussed the ideas or asked questions for comprehension, you can give them to the students as gifts. They love it! And they'll read more, too!

Magazines are also good investments. They will often have games that you can modify and use with your own students. I have found some good ones in the teachers' magazines.

There are also some good box games for teaching. *Boggle* is good for spelling. *Scrabble* is good for vocabulary. There are also games that are made for teaching math concepts.

## Teachers' Stores

Check out teachers' stores. There is a growing number of them and they carry many things you may find useful.

## Libraries

Gathering all the books and supplies you need can be costly. However, there are at least two wonderful *free* sources of material. One is the Public Library. Just think of all the possibilities. Let's say you have a student who doesn't read, and you can't seem to find out what his interests are. You can ask him to look up information just as an excuse to get him to the library so that he can look at the bookshelves crammed with every conceivable type of book. Even if he takes out books and never opens them, the library visit may be a first step. Eventually, he may start reading on his own. In addition, you can teach your students how to use the card catalog and how to tap the skills of the reference librarian.

## You Yourself!

The other free source of material is you! Granted, it takes time and energy, but actually, who knows your students' needs better than you? I had several fourth grade students who needed to learn how to do word problems in math and needed to expand their vocabulary skills. So, I wrote a story. It was all about Suzie and her desire to have a party for her friends. (See Appendix III). The first part of the story dealt with her boredom and how she decided to overcome it. I used vocabulary words and grammar rules I thought my fourth graders should know. For example, "If Suzie invited Cindy, Mary Ellen, Jane, Robert, Jonathan and Daniel Benjamin, Mike, Joan, Barbara Ann, David and Bruce, how many boys and girls did she invite?" Would my students understand the commas and count correctly?

Then I had the students help Suzie work out the costs of food, paper supplies, and decorations. Some of the problems were: If a 12-inch pizza is $4.75 and feeds 4, how many pizzas will she need to feed 12 people? (Of course, she included herself!) And how much would it cost? If plates are 8 for $0.69 or 6 for $0.49, which would be cheaper to buy? (Figure out the cost per plate.) If Suzie received a $3.00 allowance, could she pay for the food out of her saved allowances? I included addition, subtraction, multiplication and extremely easy division. Students get a big kick out of the story, especially because they know I wrote it.

Because my family's pictures are on my desk, my students know their names, and when they do work on my stories, they look to see if I have used my children or grandchildren's names in the stories.

Sometimes I make up short stories (2 or 3 paragraphs) about the students themselves. I know their likes, dislikes, pets, hobbies, etc., so it is easy and fun. I also make up my own counting games out of poster board and index cards. Each one is individualized for a particular student. If the game is a bingo game using vocabulary words, the words are the ones that student doesn't know or sight words he or she cannot read.

Use your imagination. Sometimes an idea that may sound far-fetched or too hard works out just perfectly for some student. Don't throw away ideas. Think of all the inventions that might have been tossed out if the inventor hadn't tried "just once more!"

To sum up, I must emphasize how important it is to keep an eye out for any publication you can use, whether it is a book, magazine, or newspaper. And whatever you find and wherever you see it, write down the title or source. Don't lose track of anything because some day, in some way, that bit of information may come in handy. Keep a file of publishers, games, stores, or anything that might be of use to you now and sometime in the future.

# SECTION III

# APPENDICES

# Summary of Appendices

In this section, I have printed some of the teaching aids I wrote that helped my students. You have my permission to copy them. The following are the reasons why I use them.

**Appendix 1.** This is the basic way my very young students learn to read when they are having difficulties.

**Appendix 2.** This is a lesson to help young students to follow directions.

**Appendix 3.** Suzie's story is copied here in its entirety. You may want to change prices and costs, as this was written in 1977. Students in 3rd and 4th grade work on this story.

**Appendix 4.** This is a fun way for kids to learn vocabulary.

**Appendix 5.** Many students don't understand contractions. They need to learn that the apostrophe is a place holder for either "o" in not (do not — don't) or "ha" in have (you have — you've).

**Appendix 6.** It always surprises me to find so many kids who do not know what prepositions are. They are confused by them when they need to find subjects and verbs and also when they need to locate the direct object in a sentence. And because they don't learn them well enough in elementary school, imagine the problems when they face the college entrance exams: ACT and SAT II English grammar section!

**Appendix 7.** These idioms really help students who are learning English. They need to understand that "dawn is breaking" means that it will be light soon in the mornings. And there are always some students who do speak English who don't know what the word idiom means.

**Appendix 8.** These are tips for taking the tests that you may want to give out to students.

**Appendix 9.** I give these SAT tips out to parents and students when I give speeches. I also give them to all the high school students who are studying with me.

# Appendix 1

## Teaching Basic Reading Skills

1.   Work with short vowel sounds.

2.   Make cards with words that use short vowels: for example, cap, hop, hut, bed, and pin.

3.   Make two bingo cards with simple sight words like saw, was, there, and are. Take a sheet of 8 by 10 poster board and draw a line down the middle of it. Write your students' names on the top of one side and your name on the other. Make small cards with one of the words on each of them.

   Play Bingo with your students and give the winner a star to paste under their names. They love this and it gives them the incentive to learn the words so they can win. When they know the words on the cards, make new bingo cards with new difficult words.

4.   Work on long vowels. When vowels are long, they say their own names. The first words to work with are those they already know, like hop. Add an "e" to the end of the word. Work with VCV. At becomes ate. Use an aid like "the magic e." The "e" at the end of a word doesn't make a sound but it hops back over the consonant in front of it and makes the vowel say its own name. Hop becomes hope, cap becomes cape, and Sam becomes same.

5.   Continue making bingo cards, adding words that are troubling and also new sight words.

6. Use the aid, "Two vowels go walking and the first one does the talking." Use words like read, sail, boat, and lie.

7. Be sure to teach the irregular sounds: "ei" has many sounds. Sometimes it sounds like long "a" when it says eight or sleigh or weight. Sometimes it says "i" as in height. Other times it says "e" as in receive. Another irregular sound is "ou." Sometimes "ou" sounds like "o" as in though; sometimes it sounds like "oo" like in through; it can sound like short "u" as in rough. It also can sound like "ow" like in bough or it can sound like "aw" as in cough. These words work very well on Bingo cards. There are a great many irregular words; teach them as you come to them.

8. Be sure to explain what questions marks and exclamation marks are and how to read the sentences ending with them.

9. Teach the "flat tire" letters: "kn" as in know; "gn" as in sign or gnaw: the "mb" as in climb.

10. Homonyms are fun. They're, their, and there are some. Also pear, pare, and pair.

11. You can teach antonyms by telling the kids they've been doing opposites for a long while and this is what the opposites are called. They most often already know hot and cold, up and down, tall and short. Once you put a name to this process and repeat it enough, the students will remember it.

12. You can teach synonyms by asking kids for words that mean the same thing: stout and fat; below and under; and break and crack.

13. Move up a level only when your students are reading very well in the book you are using.

# Appendix II

## Following Directions

Read each sentence and draw the right picture in each box on the following page.

1.  If you keep ice cream in the freezer, draw a star in box 6.

2.  If an elephant is smaller than a fly, draw a face in box 3.

3.  If rain helps make flowers grow, draw a house in box 2.

4.  If a car and an automobile are the same thing, write yes in box 1.

5.  If a bee can sting, draw a ball in box 4.

6.  If fish swim in lakes, write your name in box 5.

1.

2.

3.

4.

5.

6.

# Appendix III

## "Suzie Plans a Party"

Throwing herself onto a chair, Suzie muttered, "Gosh, this summer is long! Camp is over and there's nothing to do!" She stared off into space for awhile and then, suddenly, she brightened up. Scurrying to her desk, she began jotting down notes and numbers on paper, deliberating a few minutes and then crossing out some and keeping others.

Sometimes she fidgeted as she worked on her notes. Sometimes she had a furrowed brow while she wrote. Finally, she said, "Mom, I'd like to have a party. I miss the kids and I want to get together with them. If I figure out how much of everything I need and how much it will cost—and if I have enough money saved from my allowance—may I have a party? I have $17.00 altogether."

"That's a neat idea," her mother answered. "Figure out what you want, how much it costs and then we'll decide when. I'm here if you need help."

Suzie's eyes crinkled with excitement. "Thanks, Mom. I'll start right away!"

She thought for a while about whom she would invite and what she wanted to serve and then she began to plan.

On her paper Suzie wrote down guests, foods and decorations. Under girls she listed Jean, Ann Marie, Shelly, Cindy and Barbara. Under boys she listed Mike, Rich, Danny, Scott, David and Rob.

**NOTE:** *Suzie Plans a Party* was written in 1977; therefore the costs of items have greatly increased.

Then she made a chart on which she could list the items she had to buy. Under food she wrote pizzas, sodas and potato chips. Then she added paper plates, cups and napkins.

I wonder," she mused, "if it would cost much to decorate with balloons and streamers? I guess I can write them down, then see if I have enough money left over for decorations." So under decorations, she listed balloons and streamers.

Suzie now had two lists and they looked like these:

**FOOD**

| ITEM | AMOUNT TO BUY | COST |
|------|---------------|------|
| Potato Chips | 1 BOX | .59 |
| Pizzas | | |
| Sodas | | |
| Paper plates/cups | | |
| | | |

**DECORATIONS**

| ITEM | AMOUNT TO BUY | COST |
|------|---------------|------|
| Balloons | | |
| Streamers | | |
| | | |
| | | |
| | | |

"Boy, that was easy? Now it gets hard! I'll start with the easy one first. A large box of potato chips is 59 cents. One box should be enough. I can write 59 cents down on my list. (THERE'S AN EXAMPLE OF HOW YOU FIGURE OUT YOUR TOTAL COST. OKAY?)

"If a small pizza serves three people, how many pizzas do I need?"

_____

**Number of pizzas**

"If each pizza is $2.50, how much will the pizzas cost altogether?"

_____
DO YOUR FIGURING ABOVE THIS LINE AND ENTER TOTAL ON YOUR LIST.

"A large bottle of soda is $1.09," Suzie said, "and serves four people, so how many bottles of soda shall I buy?"

_____

**Number of bottles of soda needed**

"How much will all the bottles of soda cost?"

_____
DO YOUR FIGURING ABOVE THIS LINE AND ENTER TOTAL ON YOUR LIST.

## Eileen Shapiro

"Paper plates are eight for 64 cents, or ten for 70 cents. Should I buy two packages of eight, or two packages of ten? Which would be cheaper?

---

DO YOUR FIGURING ABOVE THIS LINE AND ENTER TOTAL ON YOUR LIST.

"Cups and napkins are easy," Suzie said. "Cups are 79 cents for a dozen, and napkins are 50 for 49 cents. Balloons are 20 for 59 cents a package, and streamers are 39 cents a package. (Hmmmmm, I better add up the costs of all the food first, Suzie said to herself, before I decide whether I can afford the balloons and streamers.)

Suzie did all her figuring. She added, subtracted, multiplied and divided.

When the cost of each item was figured out, she added them up to find out the total cost of the food.

> ➤ **WILL SHE HAVE ENOUGH MONEY FOR THE FOOD?**

> ➤ **WILL SUZIE HAVE ANY MONEY LEFT OVER?**

> ➤ **CAN SHE BUY ANY BALLOONS OR STREAMERS?**

Do you think you could plan a party of your own if your own Mom let you? You've learned how to do it — and you've got a right to be very proud of yourself!

**226**

# Appendix IV

On the top row a word has been printed. Change one letter of that word into a new word that fits the sentence at the right. Write in the new word and continue in the same manner.

**CURE**

1._____ to be concerned about someone (care)

2._____ to peel (pare)

3._____ to lose color in one's face (pale)

4._____ a heap of things (pile)

5._____ used to fix a broken fingernail (file)

6.__FINE___ feeling good

\* \* \* \* \* \* \* \* \* \* \* \* \* \* \* \* \* \* \* \* \* \* \* \* \* \* \* \* \* \* \* \* \* \* \* \* \* \*

**LEAK**

1._____ the tallest point (peak)

2._____ a fruit (pear)

3._____ to rip (tear)

4._____ a group of people working together (team)

5._____ the line where two pieces of material are joined together (seam)

6.__SEAR___ to burn

**227**

\* \* \* \* \* \* \* \* \* \* \* \* \* \* \* \* \* \* \* \* \* \* \* \* \* \* \* \* \* \* \* \* \* \*

**BOAT**

1._____ what one wears when it's cold (coat)

2._____ what one burns to keep warm (coal)

3._____ opposite of warm (cool)

4. _____ what a hammer is (tool)

5._____ to work hard (toil)

6.___SOIL___ to get dirty

\* \* \* \* \* \* \* \* \* \* \* \* \* \* \* \* \* \* \* \* \* \* \* \* \* \* \* \* \* \* \* \* \* \*

**SHAKE**

1._____ to use together with others (share)

2._____ to frighten (scare)

3._____ something extra (spare)

4._____ an empty place (space)

5._____ a seasoning (spice)

6.___SPINE___ one's backbone

\* \* \* \* \* \* \* \* \* \* \* \* \* \* \* \* \* \* \* \* \* \* \* \* \* \* \* \* \* \* \* \* \* \*

**PRICE**

1._____ how one feels when he's done well (pride)

2._____ first in value (prime)

3._____ an illegal act (crime)

4._____ the sound a bell makes (chime)

5._____ an ape (chimp)

6.___CHAMP___ the winner

# Appendix V

## Contractions

A contraction is made up of two words put together using an apostrophe to take the place of the letters left out. Contractions can be words like don't (do not), aren't (are not), you've (you have), they're (they are), we'll (we will), and it's (it is).

**1.** Make the following words into contractions:

is not_____ you have _____

has not_____ have not  _____

she will_____ should have _____

was not_____ you are  _____

were not_____ he is  _____

could have_____ are not  _____

do not_____ does not _____

will not (this one is kind of tricky) _____

I will _____

**2.** Use the correct word in the following sentences:

1. Yesterday we _____ gone shopping. (should have)

2. Jane _____ know where her books were. (did not)

3. _____ going to a party this afternoon. (We are)

4. We _____ take the baby with us. (will not)

5. Nellie asked where _____ going. (they are)

6. Lunch _____ ready yet. (is not)

7. _____ getting dark outside. (it is)

8. _____ left school already. (They have)

9. Bobby and Joe _____ home from the store. (Are not)

10. _____ get the art supplies we need. (She will)

# Appendix VI

## Prepositions

**1.** Prepositions are used to show the relationship of words to other words. Prepositions sometimes tell where and when. A noun or pronoun **always** follows a preposition and forms a prepositional phrase.

The mouse was *under* the steps *during* the storm.

The mouse is *near* the steps.

The mouse is *beside* the steps.

The mouse was *on* the steps *before* breakfast.

**2.** One of the best reasons for recognizing prepositional phrases in sentences is that they make it easier to determine the subjects and verbs of those sentences. For example:

One of the girls (is, are) taking ballet lessons.

Many students think *girls* is the subject so *are* is the verb, but they are mistaken. When the prepositional phrase "of the girls" is crossed out, people can easily see that *one* is the subject and *is* is the verb. Another example:

Counting points during the games (was, were) done by machine.

Cross out "during the games" and *counting* is the subject and was is the verb.

**3.** Crossing out prepositions makes it easier to find direct objects.

Studying for my exam in English exhausted me.

Eliminate "for my exam" and "in English"; *me* is the direct object.

**4.** The following are prepositions to learn:

| | | | | |
|---|---|---|---|---|
| aboard | at | down | off | underneath |
| about | before | during | on | until |
| above | behind | except | out of | up |
| across | below | for | over | upon |
| after | beneath | from | since | with |
| against | beside | in | through | within |
| along | between | into | throughout | without |
| amoung | beyond | like | to | |
| around | by | of | under | |

# Appendix VII

## Idioms

Choose correct meanings from choices below.

1. I'm sorry that you had to *cool your heels* for two hours before the dentist could see you.

2. Anyone who would walk on a building ledge one mile above the street *must have a screw loose.*

3. I can't decide whether to go along with your plan until you *put all your cards on the table.*

4. If you think I'm the boy who stole the apples, *you're barking up the wrong tree.*

5. Can you keep a secret, or will you *spill the beans?*

6. I don't know if you're telling me the truth or whether you are *full of hot air.*

7. When you told Sally that the principal was fat and ugly, you really *put your foot in your mouth.*

8. There's no choice but to *face the music.*

---

a. accept punishment ____    e. said the wrong thing ____
b. mistaken        ____    f. reveal the secret    ____
c. be crazy        ____    g. wait          ____
d. are completely   ____    h. Lying         ____
   honest

# Appendix VIII

## Tips to Prepare for Tests

1. Take notes from lectures, copy them neatly. When you study them, check points you need to review. As you read your textbook, make check marks beside those points you don't know and then review those points.

2. Use flash cards. Use your waiting time. You can study them while waiting for rides, friends and appointments.

3. Learn to differentiate between your opinions and straight facts.

4. Watch for summaries within and at the end of assigned chapters.

5. Look for bold face and italic copy. They signify important points to remember.

6. Be able to answer all the questions throughout the passages and all the questions at the ends of chapters.

7. Watch for relationships between ideas. Look for "causes and effects." Organize them logically.

8. Study in short spurts. Your mind needs intervals between absorbing materials. Long term memory occurs when learned in intervals.

9. Before a test, warm up. Scrunch up your body and then relax. Smile. You can't be tense when you sit up straight and smile. Think back to a good learning experience you had: when you learned to swim or made your first home run. Practice doing well. Tell yourself that you have done all you can (if you have) and so you will do well on the tests.

**10.** Most of all, repeat positive affirmations. "I can do it. I can get a great grade."

Henry Ford said, "If you think you can do it, you're right. If you think you can't do it, you're right."

# Appendix IX
# Tips for Taking the SAT

**SENTENCE COMPLETIONS**

**1.** Sentences that begin with contrasting words like "although, unless, rather than, despite" tell you that the first clause will be the opposite of the second.

> "Although she thought she was helping her friend in math, she was really _____ him."

**a.** teaching    **b.** clarifying    **c.** hindering
**d.** denying    **e.** eluding

The answer is **c.** hindering (opposite of helping)

**2.** Sentences that begin with words like "because, since, just as" mean that the clauses will be the same.

> "Because even the briefest period of idleness bored her, she worked _____ at some project or activity."

**a.** constantly    **b.** reluctantly    **c.** occasionally
**d.** cynically    **e.** languidly

The answer is **a.** Even the **briefest** period bored her so she couldn't be still for even a moment.

**3.** Remember — every sentence has a clue.

> "In Florida, strong winds and rain are often a(an) _____ of a hurricane that is coming."

**a.** precursor      **b.** incursion      **c.** courier
**d.** misconception  **e.** compilation

The clue is the words "a hurricane that is coming." Precursor is something that precedes an event to indicate that event is on its way.

**4.** When there are two blanks to fill in within a sentence, remember that both words must make the sentence meaningful. Sometimes it is difficult to figure out the first word but easier to determine the second word. If you do this, be sure to check the first word. They both must fit.

> "Although they are _____ by traps, poison, and shotguns, predators _____ to feed on flocks of sheep."

**a.** lured, refuse  **b.** destroyed, cease  **c.** impeded, continue
**d.** encouraged, attempt    **e.** harmed, hesitate

"Although" means look for contrasting words. The only choice with contrasting words is c. impeded, continue. Things may get in their way or harm them, but the predators still eat sheep.

## Analogies

**5.** Make up a phrase or sentence for the two words that are capitalized. Example: "COW:LOW." We hear the mooing and that sound is called lowing. Look for the same relationship in the choices. We hear sheep baaing; that sound is called bleating. So "COW:LOW:: sheep: bleat."

## Reading

**6.** Remember to do the reading passages last, after sentence completions and analogies. If one of the readings seems more difficult to understand, do the one that is easier to read first. Look for clue words like "in fact, actually, but, however." They tell you the ideas in the passage are changing from one idea to another.

**7.** When you are comparing two passages, read the first passage first, answer questions about it; then read the second and answer them the same way. Now it's easier to compare them.

## Math

**8.** Write down all your work. It's faster, easier and safer. You do not get a blue ribbon for doing math in your head and making a careless error.

**9.** A problem says that "figures are not drawn to scale." A triangle may look equilateral, but actually have three unequal sides.

It may look like this: but it could be this:

To be a right triangle, it MUST SHOW the little square where the two legs of the triangle meet or MUST SAY 90° or right triangle:

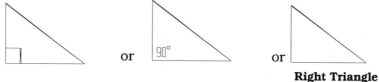

**Right Triangle**

**10.** Don't do the problems that you can't do. It's better to leave them blank rather than be penalized for wrong answers, EXCEPT ON THE STUDENT RESPONSE PROBLEMS. You get no penalty for wrong answers here; those questions answered incorrectly are considered omitted.

**11.** On the comparison problems, learn what the choices stand for.

"A" means the A column is larger than the B column.

"B" means the B column is the larger.

"C" means columns A and B are equal.

"D" means not enough information is given to determine the answer.

The following problem is an example of a "D" answer:

| Column A | Column B |
|----------|----------|
| | $n \leq 12$ |
| $4 + 5 + 12$ | $4 + 5 + n$ |

Looking at what is given, n includes all numbers from +12 down through all the negative numbers. Suppose you choose n = 12. Then Column A = Column B and your answer would be C. They are equal. BUT what if others choose n = 2? Then column A would be larger than column B and column A would be the answer. You will find there are often so many answers that there is not enough information to determine whether the answer should be A, B, or C; therefore it must be D.

You must also remember variables can be *positive*, *negative*, *zero*, or *fractions*. Use any two of them to determine unknowns.

Here is another example of a D answer.

| Column A | Column B |
|----------|----------|
| $M^5$ | $(M^2)^3$ |

Suppose M = 2, then A = 32 and B = 64, and the answer would be B. BUT if M = 1/2, then A = 1/32, B = 1/64 and A would be the answer.

**BE CAREFUL! QUANTITATIVE QUESTIONS CAN BE TRICKY!**

# INDEX

# Index

# Index

## QUESTIONS OR SUGGESTIONS?

If you have a question about tutoring, write us at Eileen Shapiro, **P.O. Box 1916, Burbank, CA 91505** or call **888-567-1926.** Enclose a self-addressed, stamped envelope or your fax number. We will respond as soon as possible. Sorry, we cannot answer detailed and involved questions.